Above the Sun:
A Prophetic Journey into God's Presence

By Eric D. Cooper

Dedication

This book is dedicated to **Brent, Wendy, Jonah, and Isaiah Wong**, and the *Shine the Light Initiative* family, in honor of the completion of home #100 built in the **El Javillar community**.

Your obedience, humility, and steadfast love have left a lasting imprint on my life and on the lives of countless others. You are a living testimony that faith expressed through love still builds hope, restores dignity, and transforms communities— one household at a time.

May the light you carry continue to shine far beyond what you can see, illuminating paths of restoration for generations to come.

To learn more about this work, visit **ShineTheLight.ca**

In Loving Memory of
John Paul Jackson
July 30, 1950 – February 18, 2015

John Paul was a mentor, teacher, and prophetic voice who shaped the way many of us learned to see, listen, and walk with God.

He taught us to live from heaven's perspective, to value truth over hype, and to carry revelation with humility and love.

This book is offered in gratitude for his life, his faithfulness, and the legacy he entrusted to us. What he helped awaken continues to bear fruit.

This book is released in loving remembrance of his life and legacy.

Contents

Acknowledgments

I am grateful to every voice, every prayer, and every faithful hand that has carried me through this journey. To my church family, friends, and mentors who stirred my faith and continually pointed me upward—thank you.

I am also thankful for voices like **Erika Kirk**, whose courage in the face of loss continues to inspire many to rise and carry the fire of faith, family, and hope, as **Charlie Kirk**'s legacy continues to ignite hearts.

Above all, I give thanks to the Holy Spirit of God—who breathed this message into me and now breathes it through these pages—calling a generation to live above the sun.

Introduction — The Weight of the World

We're living in extraordinary days. The world is trembling beneath the pressure of birth pains—headlines scream chaos, truth is mocked, and deception spreads like wildfire across the earth. Every scroll, every news alert feels designed to suffocate hope. But this is not the end. This is the beginning—the first rumblings of the greatest awakening the world has ever seen.

For too long, believers have lived *under the sun*—trapped in cycles of fear, compromise, and distraction. Life under the sun is heavy; it grinds faith down, dulls passion, and leaves souls exhausted. Yet even now, Heaven is calling us higher—*above the sun*, into the realm of His presence and glory, where the weight of the world gives way to the weight of His Spirit. This is where endurance becomes fire, intimacy becomes strength, and the Bride makes herself ready for the return of the King.

This book is not a manual. It's a scroll of awakening—a prophetic journey to pierce your heart, renew your mind, and ignite your spirit. From the weight of the world to the battle of the mind, from beholding Jesus to enduring like Joseph, aligning with Holy Spirit, and rising like Esther, these chapters trace the path from struggle to glory. You'll walk with Elijah beneath the broom tree, with David in repentance, with Esther in courage. You'll watch how each of them—under crushing pressure—rose in victory by the same Spirit who is breathing on us now.

I've lived this call.

There was a time I stood at the crossroads of comfort and consecration, when I could have drifted in lukewarm faith or burned with holy fire. In a season of confusion and noise, I heard the Spirit's whisper: *Surrender to My voice above the world's roar.*

That moment marked me forever.

It was my line in the sand.

And now, that same whisper is sounding across the earth—stirring young and old, in living rooms, on campuses, and in hidden prayer rooms—to say *yes* to the call of holiness and hope.

My prayer is that this book won't simply instruct you but ignite something eternal. May every page be a spark that draws you out of heaviness and into encounter—out of striving and into surrender. May you feel the Father's embrace, find your mind renewed, and your spirit burning again with purpose.

From the *weight of the world* to the *rewriting of your scroll*, this nine-chapter journey will lift you above the sun. The hour is urgent.

The Bridegroom is at the door. Heaven is thundering the same invitation that once shook my soul:

"Rise. Burn with holy fire. Live above the sun."

— Eric D. Cooper

Chapter 1 — The Weight of the World

Pull your chair in close. Let's sit here for a moment and feel what's really happening around us—not through the lens of panic or politics, but through Heaven's eyes. You can sense it, can't you? The heaviness that sits over the nations like a storm cloud. The noise never stops. Headlines scream division. Truth is twisted until it sounds like hate. Deception moves faster than discernment, and hope feels like it's running out of breath.

It's in moments like these that Heaven tests our perspective. Will we live *under the sun*, crushed beneath the chaos, or will we lift our eyes *above it*, where the King still reigns?

The assassination of Charlie Kirk was one of those moments that stopped time for a generation. A bold voice for truth was silenced, and a tremor ran through the Church. It felt like another weight added to an already breaking world—a blow not just to a family, but to faith itself. And yet, even as darkness tried to shout victory, another sound began to rise. It came from his widow, Erika Kirk—a sound not of vengeance, but of *forgiveness*.

In the midst of unspeakable loss, Erika stood before the world and forgave the man who murdered her husband. Her words weren't weak; they were warfare. Forgiveness became her sword. Mercy became her defiance. She said what few could imagine saying, and in that moment, the Spirit of Christ broke through the haze of grief and released something the world cannot imitate—a glory that burns *above the sun.*

I believe what we witnessed wasn't just personal courage; it was prophetic. Erika's yes became a gateway, a visible picture of the kind of love and authority the Church is being called into now. Where the world demands revenge, Heaven releases mercy. Where culture thrives on outrage, the Kingdom responds with resurrection. Her decision didn't erase the pain, but it revealed a greater reality: that even in tragedy, God is writing a redemptive story.

This is the weight of the world—it presses, it crushes, it accuses. It demands that we carry burdens never meant for our shoulders. But it's also the very pressure that reveals whether we're anchored below or lifted above.

When I heard Erika's declaration, I felt something shift in the Spirit. It was as if God was reminding us: *"The enemy can wound the body, but he cannot silence the Bride."* Out of the ashes of one family's loss, revival fire began to spread—hearts turning back to Jesus, people buying Bibles, churches filling again. The blood of the righteous still speaks, and the sound of forgiveness still breaks chains.

That's the paradox of glory. The same world that tries to crush us becomes the stage where Christ's strength is made visible. The weight of the world is real—but it is not final.

Jesus said, *"You will hear of wars and rumors of wars. See that you are not alarmed… Because lawlessness will increase, the love of many will grow cold. But the one who endures to the end will be saved. And this gospel of the kingdom will be proclaimed throughout the whole world… and then the end will come"* (Matthew 24:6, 12–14).

The end is not collapse—it's culmination. These birth pains are not proof of God's absence; they are proof of His nearness. The shaking isn't the sign of failure—it's the signal of awakening.

So, as we begin this journey together, lift your eyes higher. Don't get lost in the smoke of headlines or the roar of fear. Let your heart remember: *there is a realm above the sun,* where every tear is seen, every injustice answered, and every tragedy can still birth revival.

You were born for this hour. The same Spirit that raised Jesus from the dead lives in you. The weight of the world may press, but the weight of His glory is greater still.

Take a breath. Look up. The story is not ending—it's beginning.

Chasing Smoke Under the Sun

King Solomon, the wisest man who ever lived, looked across his empire and sighed, *"I have seen everything that is done under the sun, and behold, all is vanity and a striving after wind"* (Ecclesiastes 1:14). That line could just as easily headline today's news feed. *"Under the sun"* — that's where humanity still lives when it forgets who God is. It's the realm of endless motion and no meaning, of chasing smoke and calling it success.

That's what life under the sun feels like — like running on a treadmill of noise, reaching for something solid and watching it slip through your fingers. You scroll through your feed, and it's another argument, another scandal, another voice silenced.

You see a generation searching for purpose but finding only performance, chasing validation but discovering emptiness. It's not just them, though — we all know that ache. The exhaustion that comes from trying to hold the world together with our own hands, from searching for identity in applause that fades as quickly as it arrives.

I've been there — the grind, the pressure, the invisible race no one asked to join but everyone feels trapped in. I've built things that didn't last. I've poured energy into moments that looked meaningful but left my spirit empty. That's what Solomon meant. Under the sun, everything looks bright until you touch it — then it turns to smoke.

We live in a culture obsessed with measurement: how many followers, how many zeros on the paycheck, how many people know your name. But in that chase, the soul withers. The world offers progress without peace, motion without meaning. It tells you to hustle harder, compare deeper, and never stop proving yourself. But even when you reach the top of the mountain the world builds, the view is still gray. Because under the sun, it's all temporary — and the temporary can never fill the eternal part of you.

This is the quiet torment of our age — chasing purpose without Presence. We've traded communion for consumption, identity for image. And yet, in the middle of that exhaustion, Holy Spirit still whispers: *"Lift your eyes. This isn't your ceiling. There's life above the sun."*

Above the sun — that's where the futility breaks. That's where Solomon's lament turns to worship. There's a realm where meaning isn't measured in numbers but in nearness. Where your worth isn't what you've done but *Whose you are*. Where fruit isn't forced, it's birthed through abiding. Above the sun, everything changes — vanity becomes vision, striving melts into surrender, and exhaustion gives way to encounter.

The treadmill of this world screams, "*Run harder!*" but Heaven whispers, "*Rise higher.*"

So pause here for a moment. Breathe. Look around at the frantic pace of this culture, and ask yourself: *What am I chasing? Is it smoke, or is it substance? Is it applause, or is it the presence of God?*

Because once you taste life *above the sun*, everything else loses its grip.

Elijah's Broom Tree: God's Gentle Provision

Let's sit with Elijah for a moment—the prophet who called down fire and then collapsed in despair. The same man who faced down 850 false prophets on Mount Carmel is now found alone under a broom tree, trembling, undone. The fire had fallen, the people had shouted, "*The Lord, He is God!*" (1 Kings 18:39). Revival should have swept the land. Instead, Jezebel's threat sent him running into the wilderness, the fire on the mountain replaced by fear in the desert.

He collapses under the broom tree and whispers words that sound far too familiar: "*It is enough; now, O Lord, take away my life, for I am no better than my fathers*" (1 Kings 19:4). That's not the cry of a quitter—it's the cry of a man crushed under the weight of the world. It's what happens when the pressure to fix everything finally outweighs the strength to keep pretending you can.

Have you ever been there? Burned out from doing all the *"right"* things, but feeling like the heavens went silent? You've poured your heart into ministry, family, calling, dreams—but somewhere along the way, the fire that once fueled you flickered into embers. You find yourself saying, *"Lord, I can't keep doing this."* I've been there too—staring at the ceiling in the middle of the night, wondering if all the praying, all the pressing, all the believing has made any difference at all.

And that's where God meets Elijah—not with a rebuke, but with bread. Not with condemnation, but with comfort. *"Arise and eat, for the journey is too great for you"* (1 Kings 19:7). Those words are as tender as they are true. The angel doesn't scold him for feeling weak; he simply feeds him and lets him rest. It's the Father's way—when the world's weight crushes you, He doesn't pile on guilt; He prepares a table.

It's here—under the broom tree—that the rhythm of striving breaks. Elijah's body collapses, but his spirit begins to reset. God isn't done with him; He's recalibrating him. Before there can be fresh fire on Mount Horeb, there must be rest in the wilderness. And maybe that's where you are right now—not in rebellion, but recovery. You're not losing faith; you're shedding exhaustion. Heaven isn't mad at you; Heaven's baking bread for you.

When Elijah finally ate, drank, and rested, Scripture says he was strengthened *"by that food forty days and forty nights"* (1 Kings 19:8). One divine meal sustained him through an entire journey. That's the power of God's presence—it doesn't just satisfy; it sustains.

Maybe you've been chasing smoke under the sun, and all it's left you with is spiritual fatigue. The broom tree becomes God's mercy—a place to stop, breathe, and be fed again. Because before God sends you back into the battle, He'll always call you into rest. Before the roar, there's the whisper. Before the mountain, there's the meal. And that's how the weight begins to lift—not by your striving, but by His sustaining.

So if you find yourself under your own broom tree tonight—tired, disillusioned, done—don't mistake it for an ending. It's an altar. It's where God lays out bread for your spirit and whispers, *"The journey is not over. You are not forgotten. Arise, and eat."*

This is where strength returns. This is where endurance is reborn. This is where the fire that once fell on the mountain begins to burn in you again.

Israel Under Pharaoh: Breaking the Chains

Let's walk a little further together—this time into Egypt's heat, where the sound of cracking whips drowns out the songs of freedom. Israel—God's covenant people—were meant for promise, but they'd been pressed into slavery. Brick by brick, they built monuments they'd never inhabit, cities that carried no trace of their name. The Pharaoh of their day wasn't just a man; he was a system—a spirit that demanded endless output but offered no rest. It was the ancient face of the same spirit that drives our culture now.

Every sunrise brought the same demand: *"Make more bricks."* That's the gospel of the world—perform, produce, prove. Pharaoh never hands you freedom; he only raises your quota. His chains aren't always made of iron; most are invisible. Debt, comparison, exhaustion, self-worth measured by output—those are his new shackles. Egypt doesn't look like pyramids anymore. It looks like burnout. It sounds like anxiety. It feels like a soul stretched too thin to pray.

Israel groaned under that weight. Scripture says, *"The people of Israel groaned because of their slavery and cried out for help. Their cry for rescue from slavery came up to God"* (Exodus 2:23). Those cries still rise today—from weary parents trying to make ends meet, from leaders crushed beneath expectations, from young people told their worth is measured in clicks and followers. But here's the truth Pharaoh never wants you to remember: the moment you cry out, Heaven moves.

"And God heard their groaning, and God remembered His covenant with Abraham, with Isaac, and with Jacob. God saw the people of Israel—and God knew" (Exodus 2:24–25). God knew. He didn't just observe their pain; He felt it. He didn't just acknowledge their suffering; He stepped into it. The covenant wasn't forgotten—it was activated. That's how deliverance always begins. Before Moses ever stood before Pharaoh, before miracles ever split the Red Sea, there was a cry that pierced Heaven.

So let me ask you: have you heard Pharaoh's voice—the one that whispers, *"You're only as valuable as your output"*? It's subtle, but relentless. It pushes you harder, faster, longer, until you can't tell the difference between purpose and performance. Maybe you've listened to that voice for so long it feels normal. But what if the Spirit of God is whispering something different right now—something that cuts through the noise: *"No more bricks."*

What if this is the moment you remember who you really are—not a slave defined by production, but a son or daughter known by presence? Not a laborer building someone else's empire, but a priest building altars for His glory?

Pharaoh's system cannot withstand Heaven's covenant. When God sends a deliverer, the order of the world begins to tremble. It happened then, and it's happening now. He's still raising deliverers—voices that carry His heart into places of oppression, intercessors who break spiritual chains, sons and daughters who refuse to bow to the metrics of Babylon. These are the Moses generation of our hour—those who will stand before the systems of this world and declare, *"Let My people go."*

Maybe you've been living under Pharaoh's lash without realizing it—pressured, anxious, running hard but getting nowhere. If so, this is your exodus moment. The Father is whispering, *"You don't belong in Egypt anymore. You were made for promise. You were made for Me."*

The same God who broke Pharaoh's chains is breaking yours. The same fire that burned in the bush burns now within your spirit. The same voice that called Moses is calling you—to come out, to live free, to rise above the sun where His presence is your promised land.

Because what the world calls bondage, Heaven calls preparation. And the groans of captivity? They're always the sound of deliverance being born.

The Weight of Glory: A Greater Story

There's a moment when the noise quiets—when, after the groaning and the struggle, Heaven pulls back the veil and lets you see. What felt like endless labor in Egypt suddenly reveals itself as preparation. What you thought was breaking you was actually building you for glory.

Paul understood this mystery when he wrote, *"This light momentary affliction is preparing for us an eternal weight of glory beyond all comparison, as we look not to the things that are seen but to the things that are unseen"* (2 Corinthians 4:17–18).

Pause there: *an eternal weight of glory.*

Do you hear it? The same word—*weight*—that once described the oppression of Pharaoh now describes the glory of God. The enemy presses down to crush, but God presses in to transform. What the world calls heavy, Heaven calls holy.

The difference is in where your eyes rest.

Under the sun, all you see is the visible—conflict, politics, inflation, betrayal, exhaustion. It's like standing in a fog and calling it reality. But lift your gaze above the sun, and suddenly you see the mountain behind the mist. You see that pain has purpose. You see that affliction isn't final. You see that glory has been gathering around your life, even in the darkest nights.

That's the invitation of this hour: to trade the temporary for the eternal. The world shouts, *"Fix your eyes on what's urgent!"* Heaven whispers, *"Fix your eyes on what's unseen."*

Because unseen doesn't mean unreal—it means eternal. The unseen realm is more solid than everything we can touch. It's where your scroll was written, where your purpose was spoken, where your tears are counted, and where your crown is waiting.

Maybe you've carried something that feels unbearable—a loss, a betrayal, a delay you can't explain. You've wondered, *"Lord, where are You in this?"* The answer isn't that He's distant; it's that He's deep. He's not standing apart from your pain; He's weighting it with glory.

When the furnace feels hottest, He's not punishing you—He's refining you for inheritance. When you feel unseen, He's writing chapters that can only be read above the sun.

Every story Heaven writes has this rhythm: groaning, glory, gratitude. The Israelites groaned in bondage; the Red Sea split; songs of deliverance filled the night. Elijah groaned beneath the broom tree; glory whispered through the still, small voice. Jesus groaned in Gethsemane; resurrection thundered three days later.

So what if what you're feeling right now—the heaviness, the disillusionment, the ache—isn't the end, but the turning of the page? What if the very pressure meant to break you is the birthplace of weighty glory that will outlast every storm?

The world's weight enslaves, but Heaven's weight sets free. The world's weight exhausts, but Heaven's weight transforms.

When you live above the sun, the very affliction that tried to destroy you becomes the forge that prepares you for glory.

This is the invitation of *Above the Sun*—to lift your eyes beyond the transient, beyond the scroll of headlines, into the eternal scroll of His purpose. The Spirit of God is calling you to see differently: not through the lens of fear, but through the lens of glory. Because when your eyes fix on Jesus, the pressure shifts. The world loses its hold, and eternity takes its place.

The weight of the world is real, but the weight of glory is greater.

And once you've seen that, you can never live the same again.

No Room for Lukewarm

There's a fire moving through the earth right now—not the fire of destruction, but the fire of decision. It's burning through every gray place, every divided heart, every fence we've tried to balance on between the world and the kingdom. The Spirit of God is drawing a line in the sand, and every follower of Jesus must choose which side of the flame they'll stand on.

Jesus' words to Laodicea still thunder across time: *"I know your works: you are neither cold nor hot. Would that you were either cold or hot! So, because you are lukewarm, and neither hot nor cold, I will spit you out of My mouth."* (Revelation 3:15–16)

Lukewarm isn't a temperature—it's a condition of the heart. It's the slow drift from dependence into self-sufficiency, the polite faith that prays without expectation and worships without surrender. It's a Christianity that looks alive but has no pulse of Presence. Lukewarmness sings the songs but resists the fire. It nods at the cross but avoids the cost.

And yet, the hour we're living in will not permit neutrality. The world's shaking, deception's deepening, persecution's rising—and the Spirit is calling forth those who burn. Lukewarm faith won't survive this shaking. It cracks under pressure, because it's built on comfort, not conviction. But hearts set ablaze by love will stand when everything else trembles.

Maybe you've felt that tension—your faith flickering between passion and apathy. You love Jesus, but the world's pull feels strong. You've been weary, distracted, running on spiritual fumes. The truth is, we've all known that drift. It happens quietly, in the spaces between revival and routine. But even now, Jesus is knocking again. *"Behold, I stand at the door and knock. If anyone hears My voice and opens the door, I will come in to him and eat with him, and he with Me."* (Revelation 3:20)

Can you sense it? That knock isn't condemnation—it's invitation. It's the King Himself asking to reignite the flame. He doesn't shame the weary; He awakens the willing. He's not looking for perfection; He's looking for hearts that still burn when the world grows cold.

- This is the hour to stir the embers.
- To return to first love.
- To choose fire over comfort, devotion over distraction, surrender over safety.

Because the lukewarm spirit isn't just complacent—it's contagious. It numbs the Church into silence while culture roars. It dims the light that was meant to expose darkness. But the flame of devotion—one heart wholly surrendered—can ignite a thousand others. When one believer catches fire, entire families, cities, and nations feel the heat. And so, Heaven asks again: *Will you burn?* Will you let the fire of His love consume every idol, every compromise, every secret half-measure? Will you live for something that cannot be shaken?

The Bridegroom is coming, and He's not returning for a lukewarm bride. He's coming for one who's radiant with oil, blazing with affection, awake and watching. This isn't a call to hype—it's a call to holiness. It's a call to hearts that burn clean and steady, not because of willpower, but because they've been captured by love.

The world needs believers who shine, not blend. Prophets who weep, not posture. Intercessors who carry the weight of nations in prayer. Worshippers who tremble at His word more than they chase applause. This is the fire that purifies. This is the flame that overcomes.

The question is no longer *Can you endure the heat?* but *Can you afford to live without it?* Because in the days ahead, living above the sun won't be optional—it will be the only way to survive. The Spirit is whispering again, clear and steady: *"Choose fire. Choose Me."* The lukewarm will fade with the world they've tried to please. But those who burn will shine forever.

The Prophetic Edge We Can't Ignore

Lukewarm faith will not survive the days ahead. The shaking that's begun is exposing every divided heart, stripping away every mask of comfort religion has worn. The fire of God is searching, separating, refining. And what's emerging is a remnant—men and women who will not bow to fear, not compromise under pressure, not trade conviction for convenience.

The assassination of Charlie Kirk was more than tragedy—it was a prophetic flare lighting up the battle lines in this generation.

It exposed the antichrist spirit that seeks to silence truth-tellers, to intimidate those who carry the light. But out of that same moment, a spark ignited—a sound that can't be muted. Erika's forgiveness became a gateway, a visible picture of what true authority looks like: love that conquers hate, mercy that dismantles darkness.

Can you sense it? Something is stirring beneath the headlines—something Heaven-breathed. A holy unrest in young hearts. Prayer meetings in school gyms. Worship breaking out in dorm rooms. Families gathering again around living room altars. These aren't isolated moments; they're tremors of an awakening that's already begun. Holy Spirit is moving in the margins, calling the hidden ones to stand, to speak, to shine. This is not the time to drift or to blend in. The age of casual Christianity is ending. The middle ground is disappearing. You cannot straddle the world and the kingdom any longer—neutrality is surrender, and apathy is agreement with the enemy.

The Spirit is drawing a clear line of fire through the Church, and only those who burn with holy love will stand unshaken. The darkness is deepening—but those who carry the weight of glory will walk steady through trembling nations. They will be light in the ruins, peace in the storm, and fire in the cold. The weight of the world is heavy, but His glory is heavier, and it's pulling you upward.

Revival's Rising, and So Is the Fire

The harvest is not coming—it's here. We are standing on the threshold of a billion-soul awakening, prophesied for decades and now breaking into reality.

It's not organized, branded, or man-led. It's the wildfire of the Spirit, moving through surrendered hearts, crossing denominations, nations, and generations.

You can feel it—baptisms in rivers and oceans, worship erupting on campuses, spontaneous prayer gatherings where no one cares who leads, only Who is present. Teenagers falling to their knees, families praying through the night, churches overflowing with hunger that no structure can contain. This isn't hype—it's holiness. It's the groan of creation answered by the roar of revival.

But don't be naïve: the fire that awakens also tests. The same shaking that breaks chains exposes compromise. As in Egypt, Jezebel's court, and Rome's prisons, the systems of this world will push back. Darkness always resists the dawn. Casual faith will not hold under this heat. Only those anchored above the sun—those whose lives are built on unseen glory—will endure. The shaking is mercy. It's Heaven's way of removing what cannot last so that what is eternal might remain. The same hand that exposes lukewarmness is the hand preparing a pure Bride, burning away fear, refining love, and filling lamps with oil for the days ahead.

The Bride Made Ready

Scripture declares: *"The Bride has made herself ready."* (Revelation 19:7) This isn't poetic imagery—it's prophecy. The Spirit is clothing the Church in holiness again. Every compromise is being confronted. Every double allegiance is being stripped away. The call is going out: *Trim your lamps. Keep your oil. Stay awake.* The Bride is being purified by fire. She is learning to love without mixture, to burn without burnout, to worship without wavering. This is not the hour for polished religion or borrowed passion. It's the hour to be undone in His presence, to carry a flame that refuses to go out. The shaking is intensifying because the Groom is near. Persecution will rise. Pressure will mount. But for those who live above the sun, the same fire that consumes the world will refine their hearts.

The Spirit who fed Elijah beneath the broom tree, who broke Pharaoh's chains, who walked with Paul through storms and prisons, is breathing on you now. You are not called merely to survive this hour—you are anointed to shine through it. You were never meant to hide from the dark, but to set it ablaze.

A Vision for This Hour

I see it prophetically in the Spirit—a generation rising from the ashes of confusion and compromise. Unbowed by Babylon's lies. Unshaken by Jezebel's threats. Unbroken by Pharaoh's demands. Their eyes burn with eternity; their hearts pulse with holy defiance. They are the Daniels of this age—faithful in exile, radiant in courage. They are the Esthers—standing before kings, risking everything for truth. They are the Elijahs—calling down fire in the midst of drought. These are not celebrity Christians. They are the nameless and faceless ones—hidden in prayer rooms, worshipping in silence, carrying revival in the secret place. The world won't always see them, but Heaven knows their names. They are the ones carrying oil in an hour of scarcity, fire in an age of compromise. And the Spirit of God is whispering again, clear as thunder: *"This is your hour of decision. Will you live crushed under the world's weight, or will you rise into the weight of My glory? Will you settle for lukewarm comfort, or will you burn with holy fire? The time is short. The King is near."*

This is not fear—it's invitation. What crushes others will refine you if you live above the sun. The shaking that terrifies the world will strengthen you if your heart is anchored in glory. You are being prepared for something eternal—for a Bridegroom who is coming soon.

Lift your eyes. Shake off the dust. The hour is late, but the glory is rising. Step out of the shadows and into the fire. Carry His flame. Live above the sun. Because the King is coming—and He's training your mind and heart to endure.

Chapter 2 — The Battle of the Mind

The War Within—The Mind as Battleground

Friend, the greatest war you'll ever face isn't fought on a battlefield or in the streets — it's fought between your ears.

Every thought is a seed, every agreement a gate, every imagination a construction site where destinies are either built or destroyed. This is the battleground of your mind — the unseen arena where heaven and hell contend for your focus, your peace, and your identity.

Walk with me here—not as a teacher lecturing, but as a companion under the same stars, tracing the quiet war that rages inside us all. The greatest battles of your life will never be fought in headlines or on social media; they'll be fought in the stillness of your thought life, where every whisper has the power to anchor heaven or empower hell.

The world we see in chaos is only the outflow of minds unguarded and hearts unanchored. Every war, every division, every deception first began as a thought whispered in the dark. That's why the enemy works overtime to colonize your mind—because whoever shapes your thoughts, steers your life. Proverbs 23:7 says it plainly: *"As a man thinks in his heart, so is he."*

Look around. We scroll, swipe, and absorb without pause. Devices glow like miniature pulpits, preaching sermons of fear, outrage, and comparison to an entire generation. The result is exactly what Paul foresaw: *"In the last days there will come times of difficulty… people will be lovers of self, lovers of money, proud, arrogant… lovers of pleasure rather than lovers of God.”* (2 Timothy 3:1–4)

This is the mind under siege—a battlefield lit by screens and fought in silence. But here's the hope—the Spirit of God is reclaiming territory inside of you. Every anxious thought, every false identity, every echo of shame that's lingered for years is being confronted by truth. This isn't about positive thinking; it's about prophetic alignment—learning to think from heaven's perspective. It's about replacing the world's soundtrack of fear with the sound of the Father's voice. It's about silencing the chatter of hell until the whisper of Heaven becomes your first instinct. Because the battle of the mind isn't a self-help struggle; it's a spiritual war. And you can't win it through willpower. You win it through surrender. You win it by letting truth—not opinion, not emotion, not culture— define reality again.

Paul laid out the battle plan when he wrote, *"For though we walk in the flesh, we are not waging war according to the flesh. The weapons of our warfare are not of the flesh but have divine power to destroy strongholds. We destroy arguments and every lofty opinion raised against the knowledge of God, and take every thought captive to obey Christ."* (2 Corinthians 10:3–5) That means your mind is not a playground; it's a gate. You get to decide what enters and what stays. You can't always control which thoughts arrive, but you can decide which ones get to build a home. Think of it this way—your mind is either a throne or a battlefield. If you enthrone truth, peace reigns. If you entertain lies, warfare never ends. Every time you agree with fear, you empower it. Every time you agree with truth, you disarm hell.

Strongholds don't appear overnight. They begin as whispers you don't challenge, questions you replay, assumptions you let harden into truth. One unguarded thought becomes a brick; bricks become walls; walls become prisons. But the same Word that exposes them carries the power to tear them down.

The shaking of the world is exposing not just what we believe, but how we think. You can't walk in peace with a storm inside your mind. You can't carry glory while feeding on garbage. You can't rise above the sun while your thoughts are chained to the dust. The invitation is simple but costly: *"Be transformed by the renewal of your mind."* (Romans 12:2)

Transformation isn't about behavior—it's about alignment. It's not what you do that changes first—it's what you believe.

When truth renews your mind, your actions follow effortlessly. When lies hold your mind hostage, you can pray, serve, even preach—and still live like a slave. This is the war of our generation—the unseen front line that determines every visible outcome.

And this is the battleground we're walking through together; how to think above the sun. How to pull down the strongholds that have built castles in your mind. How to trade anxiety for authority, confusion for clarity, striving for surrender. Because the war of our age isn't fought with swords or slogans—it's fought with agreement. And whoever wins your agreement, wins your future.

The war is real, but so is your weaponry. You're not fighting for victory—you're fighting from it.

The Spirit within you carries divine demolition power, ready to shatter every lie that has claimed territory in your thoughts.

This is your moment to reclaim the throne of your mind and let the King of Glory reign there again.

Eden's Whisper: The First Battle

Let's walk back to the beginning—to a garden still dripping with dew, where heaven and earth once spoke the same language.

The air was pure, unpolluted by fear, untouched by shame. Adam and Eve walked with God in the cool of the day—Spirit to spirit, thought to thought, heart to heart. There was no striving, no suspicion, no separation. It was perfect communion. Until a whisper broke the silence.

"Did God really say…?" (Genesis 3:1)

No army marched into Eden that day. No sword was drawn. The first war began not with violence, but with a voice—a question planted like a seed in the soil of Eve's mind. The serpent didn't challenge God's power; he challenged His character. It was the first psychological war—the first propaganda campaign. That's how deception always begins— not with open rebellion, but with subtle distortion. The enemy didn't need to attack the garden; he only needed to infiltrate Eve's thoughts.

The lie came wrapped in logic: *"God's holding out on you. He knows if you eat, you'll be like Him."* (Genesis 3:5) But here's the tragedy—she already was like Him.

Formed in His image, clothed in His glory, walking in His presence—yet one suggestion of lack created a world of doubt.

It's the same tactic today. The serpent still whispers through screens, through ideologies, through exhaustion and shame:

"Did God really say you're loved?"

"Did He really say purity matters?"

"Did He really mean He'll provide?"

"Maybe you need to take control. Maybe you need more."

The war for Eden is the war for your mind. Because before Eve reached for the fruit, she reached for an idea. Before her hands sinned, her thoughts did. Every fall begins with agreement. And every agreement begins with a whisper. That's why the battle for your thoughts is the battle for your future.

The enemy doesn't need to destroy you if he can distract you. He doesn't need to possess your body if he can persuade your mind. Notice what the serpent didn't say—he never denied God existed; he just distorted His tone. That's his favorite trick: to twist truth until it sounds reasonable but feels wrong. To make rebellion look like freedom. To make self-rule sound like wisdom. But here's the redemption hidden in the ruin: the same battlefield where humanity fell is where Christ won it back.

In the wilderness, Satan used the same tactic on Jesus: *"If You are the Son of God…"* (Matthew 4:3)

It was Eden all over again—but this time, the Second Adam didn't reason with the lie. He rebuked it. *"It is written…"*—three words that split the serpent's tongue in half. Every *"It is written"* you declare pulls your mind back into divine order. Every agreement with truth rebuilds what the lie tried to dismantle. Every time you refuse to entertain the whisper, you reclaim the garden of your thoughts for God's glory. And maybe that's where the Spirit is meeting you right now—not in guilt, but in invitation.

To pause.

To listen.

To ask: *What whispers have I allowed to shape me?*

Which questions have I replayed until they became truth?

Because Eden wasn't lost in a day. It was lost in a moment of agreement. And every moment of agreement can be redeemed by a greater truth. The serpent still whispers, but the blood still speaks louder. The war for your mind isn't over, but the victory's already been secured. Now it's your turn to walk it out—to take back what the enemy stole, one thought at a time, one *"It is written"* at a time, until the garden of your mind blooms again with the sound of His voice.

Elijah's Fear: When Lies Feel Like Truth

Let's step forward from Eden's whisper into the desert wind—where another voice, just as cunning, tries to undo a prophet. Elijah had just called down fire from heaven. The people fell on their faces. False prophets were silenced. Revival, it seemed, was finally breaking through the clouds. But then came a message—short, sharp, and venomous.

Jezebel sent word: *"So may the gods do to me and more also, if I do not make your life as one of them by this time tomorrow."* (1 Kings 19:2)

That's all it took. A single threat. And the man who had just outrun chariots crumbled. Elijah fled into the wilderness, collapsing under a broom tree, whispering, *"It is enough; now, O Lord, take away my life."* (v. 4) He wasn't physically wounded; he was mentally crushed. His mind had turned on him. Fear had taken Jezebel's hiss and built it into a fortress of despair.

That's how the enemy operates. He doesn't need to touch your body if he can torment your thoughts. He doesn't need to imprison your limbs if he can convince you you're already trapped. The prophet who had just seen heaven open now felt completely alone. *"I, even I only, am left…"* (v. 10) That's the lie—you're alone. It's the same whisper that echoes in our generation: *No one understands you. No one stands with you. You're fighting a losing battle. You're the last one still believing.* And if you let that lie linger long enough, it will sound like truth. But then—listen— God doesn't rebuke Elijah's exhaustion. He meets it. He sends an angel, carrying bread and water, and says simply, *"Arise and eat, for the journey is too great for you."* (v. 7)

That's the Father's voice in your own wilderness. Not, "Get over it." Not, "Where's your faith?" Just, *"Rest. Eat. Let Me strengthen you."* He knows the journey's long. He knows how heavy the call feels. But He also knows the whisper of truth still waiting to rise within you.

When Elijah finally reached the mountain, God didn't thunder or quake; He whispered. And that whisper shattered the lie.

Elijah wasn't the last. He wasn't forsaken. God had seven thousand more who hadn't bowed to Baal. (v. 18)

What if the same is true for you?

What if the voices in your head aren't reporting reality, but replaying fear? What if your exhaustion isn't failure, but a setup for fresh encounter? Because when God whispers, He's not trying to match the volume of the lie—He's restoring intimacy. He's reminding you that the same still, small voice that spoke light into chaos still speaks peace into your storm.

He's reminding you that your perception is not your truth, and your fear is not your future. Elijah's story is proof: you can be anointed and still feel afraid. You can be obedient and still feel empty. But if you'll stay in the wilderness long enough to hear His whisper, the lie will break, and the mission will resume.

There's a generation right now—prophetic, fiery, anointed—but weary. They've seen God move in power, but Jezebel's voice has worn them down. To them, and maybe to you, the Spirit says: *"Eat again. Drink again. Hear Me again."*

The battle of the mind doesn't end when the fire falls—it begins when the whisper returns. And in that whisper, you'll find your strength. You'll remember you're not alone.

And you'll rise, above the sun, with a renewed mind ready to tear down strongholds.

The Renewed Mind: Your Path to Transformation

When Elijah stepped out of the cave and wrapped his mantle around his face, everything changed. The storm didn't disappear. Jezebel didn't repent. The threats didn't stop. But Elijah was no longer ruled by them. Something had shifted inside—his perspective. That's what a renewed mind does: it doesn't erase the battle; it redefines it. The circumstances may look the same, but your position changes—from victim to victor, from confusion to clarity, from survival to assignment.

Paul understood this better than anyone. Writing to the believers in Rome—people living in the shadow of emperors and idols—he gave a command that still cuts through centuries of noise:

"Do not be conformed to this world, but be transformed by the renewal of your mind, that by testing you may discern what is the will of God, what is good and acceptable and perfect." —Romans 12:2

Notice the progression—**conformed** or **transformed**.

There's no neutral ground. You're either being shaped by the world or renewed by the Word. The culture around you is not passive—it's persuasive. It's constantly pressing, molding, and whispering: *Be more like us. Think like us. Love what we love. Fear what we fear.* And without realizing it, conformity begins to feel like comfort. But Paul says transformation begins when you refuse to think like Egypt, when you stop letting Pharaoh rent space in your imagination.

The renewed mind is not self-improvement; it's spiritual revolution. It's when Heaven's logic becomes your default, when truth overrules trauma, and when peace outruns panic.

Transformation doesn't start with your habits; it starts with your agreements. You can change your routine but still carry the same mental architecture. You can attend church, sing the songs, pray the prayers—and still think like a slave. But when truth renews your mind, your actions follow without strain.

You stop trying to behave better and start believing differently. Think about it—Elijah's fear didn't lift because Jezebel disappeared. It lifted because his perspective shifted.

The cave became a classroom, and the whisper rewired his thinking. He came out of hiding carrying the same mantle, but now it rested on a renewed mind. And that's what God is doing in you. He's rewriting the inner script that's defined your identity. He's teaching you to see beyond the chaos of this world to the Kingdom that cannot be shaken. He's reminding you that the greatest transformation happens not when you escape pressure—but when your mind stops agreeing with it.

Have you ever noticed how the mind wants to fix what only God can heal?

We analyze, replay, worry, and plan, as if anxiety could produce peace. But transformation begins where self-sufficiency ends. It's when you say, *"Lord, I don't just need You to change my situation; I need You to change how I see it."*

Renewal is not about escaping your thoughts—it's about *redeeming* them. It's about allowing Holy Spirit to inhabit the places fear once ruled. It's about making space for His truth to replace the narratives that have kept you bound.

So pause for a moment.

Where have you been conforming—squeezed by pressure, bent by expectation, dulled by distraction? And where is the Spirit calling you to transform—to rise above the noise, to think from Heaven's perspective, to align with His will again? Because this is more than mindset—it's mission. A renewed mind is the foundation for a renewed life. And a renewed life becomes a testimony that lights up dark places. You can't carry revival while thinking like a slave. You can't discern God's will while agreeing with the world's lies. But the moment your mind bows to truth, everything begins to shift.

The renewed mind isn't just a personal victory—it's a prophetic weapon. It's how you pull down strongholds without shouting, how you silence the enemy without striving. It's the quiet revolution of a believer who sees through Heaven's eyes and walks through Hell's noise unshaken. That's what this chapter is preparing you for—not just a new mindset, but a new way of living *above the sun*. Because the battle for your mind isn't only about what you think—it's about *who you become*. And when your mind is renewed, your life becomes the sermon.

How Strongholds Take Root

If the renewed mind is a garden, then a stronghold is the weed that refuses to die. It begins quietly, underground—a whisper beneath the surface, a thought that seems harmless enough. But if left unchallenged, it grows roots deep into your identity. Before long, what started as a passing idea becomes a pattern of belief, and that pattern begins to shape everything you see.

Paul's word for *stronghold* in 2 Corinthians 10:4 wasn't poetic—it was strategic. A stronghold is a fortress, a walled city in the mind, built brick by brick through repetition and agreement. It is not built overnight. It is built every time you agree with something God never said.

The enemy doesn't need to overpower you; he just needs you to agree with him. He knows he can't steal your calling, so he tries to distort your confidence. He can't rewrite your scroll, but he will whisper until you start doubting what's written on it. And once you agree with the lie, he lets you build the wall yourself.

Strongholds always start with a seed—a thought.

Maybe it begins as, *"I'll never change."*
Then it becomes a conversation: *"Why even try?"*
Then an identity: *"This is just who I am."*

Brick by brick, it forms a fortress.

The tragedy is that most believers don't even realize they're living inside one. You can attend church, sing about freedom, even preach liberty to others—and still be locked inside a mental prison that you helped construct.

That's why Paul doesn't say we ignore strongholds; he says we destroy them. We pull them down. We break agreement. We bring every thought—every brick—into obedience to Christ.

Because every thought left unsubmitted becomes a gateway for deception.

Let's name how they form — and how they fall:

Step 1: Agreement — The Whisper Becomes Familiar.

The serpent never shouts; he suggests.

"You're not enough."
"God's holding out on you."
"Nothing's really changing."

The first brick is laid the moment you nod—even silently—
and let that whisper linger.

Step 2: Argument — The Lie Begins to Justify Itself

Once the whisper settles, the mind starts building logic
around it.

If God really loved me, He would've answered by now.
If I was truly called, it wouldn't be this hard.

Now the lie isn't just believed—it's defended. You start
explaining your chains as if they're natural, excusing what
you were meant to evict.

Step 3: Identity — The Lie Takes the Throne

What began as a thought becomes a name tag.

"I'm anxious."
"I'm broken."
"I'm a failure."

No, you're not. Those are walls talking.

The longer you listen, the higher the fortress grows—until you mistake the prison for your personality.

But here's the good news: strongholds aren't eternal.

They crumble under truth.
They shake when light enters.
They fall when you stop defending them and start declaring war against them.

You can't counsel a stronghold out; you have to confront it.
You can't medicate it away; you must evict it through truth.

Because *"the weapons of our warfare are not of the flesh, but have divine power to demolish strongholds"* (2 Corinthians 10:4).

Every time you declare what God says instead of what fear says, a wall cracks.
Every time you forgive instead of replaying the wound, a brick falls.
Every time you worship in the face of despair, a gate swings open.

Truth doesn't just inform you—it transforms you.

Have you ever noticed that the enemy's lies always sound like your own thoughts? That's because he's a mimic, not a creator. He imitates your voice to make you believe it's you talking.

But the renewed mind begins to discern the difference between conviction and accusation.

Conviction always points you back to Christ.
Accusation always points you back to yourself.

So pause for a moment and ask:

What are the walls in my mind made of? Comparison? Shame? Fear? Self-hatred?

And who taught me to build them?

Now imagine Holy Spirit walking those same corridors—light streaming through the cracks, His voice gentle but sure:

"This wall doesn't belong here anymore."

He's not angry that you built it. He's simply ready to take it down.

And the weapon He wields is truth.

Because strongholds don't fall by accident—they fall by agreement.

When you agree with Heaven, hell's scaffolding collapses. When you say, *"No more lies. No more fear. No more agreement with defeat,"* the fortress begins to crumble from the inside out.

Suddenly, what once felt like a prison becomes a gateway into freedom.

You realize you were never powerless—you were just partnered with the wrong voice.

The renewed mind isn't just about new thoughts; it's about new ownership.

Your mind doesn't belong to anxiety, to shame, or to the world's narrative. It belongs to the Spirit of Truth who lives within you. And when He takes possession, every false fortress must bow.

So let the demolition begin.

Brick by brick.
Lie by lie.

The ruins of your old thinking will make way for something new—a mind anchored above the sun, where peace reigns, truth governs, and glory fills every room.

Gideon: From Hiding to Holy Fire

Somewhere in the hills of Israel, a man named Gideon was hiding.

Not in sin.
Not in rebellion.
In fear.

He was threshing wheat in a winepress—the wrong place, the wrong tool, the wrong season—because the Midianites had stripped Israel of courage. They raided crops, burned fields, and stole faith. Gideon hid what little he had left, trying to survive.

If you've ever lived through disappointment, you know this posture well.

When loss lingers, when prayers go unanswered, when hope feels mocked, you start threshing in secret. You go through the motions of faith while wondering if God still sees you.

You keep embers alive beneath the surface, afraid the next gust might extinguish them.

And then—into that hiding place—heaven interrupts.

"The Lord is with you, O mighty man of valor." (Judges 6:12)

What a greeting.

Gideon isn't being heroic. He's just surviving. Yet God calls him mighty.

Because Heaven doesn't speak to your circumstance—it speaks to your calling. It doesn't name you by what you're doing; it names you by what you're destined for.

But Gideon can't receive it yet.

He answers with the honesty of a weary soul:

"If the Lord is with us, why has all this happened to us?" (Judges 6:13)

It's a question as old as pain.

Why, God?
Why me?
Why now?

Maybe that's where you are—buried in a season that feels beneath your potential, wondering why Heaven's promises haven't matched earth's reality.

But what if God hasn't abandoned you—He's hiding you?

What if the winepress isn't punishment, but preparation?
Not rejection, but refinement?
Not delay, but design?

Gideon's story isn't about a man who found courage. It's about a man who encountered Presence.

He lays down an offering, and fire consumes it.

Fear meets fire.

For the first time, Gideon isn't defined by what's been taken from him—he's defined by the One who called him.

That's where deliverance begins: when the voice of truth burns louder than the echo of fear.

The same pattern plays out today.

Fear builds winepresses in our minds—places where we hide our gifting, our boldness, our faith.

You hear it in phrases like:

"It's not the right time."
"Someone else is more qualified."
"I've failed too many times."

Those are winepress words—survival language spoken under pressure.

But God still walks into those places, calling you by names that don't match your posture.

Mighty one.
Warrior.

Deliverer.
Voice of freedom.

And when you begin to agree—even tremblingly—the fire
falls.

Because the moment you stop arguing with your old identity,
your new one begins to live.

Gideon tore down idols in the night—afraid, but obedient.
He confronted the altar within before confronting the enemy
without.

Fear broke.

He didn't become fearless; he became faith-full.

Then came the battle.

Thirty-two thousand answered the call, but God reduced
them to three hundred.

Three hundred jars.
Three hundred torches.
Three hundred trumpets.

Against an army like sand.

It made no sense—unless you looked above the sun.

Because in God's arithmetic, less is often more. He doesn't
multiply by addition; He multiplies by surrender.

When Gideon's band broke their jars and lifted their torches,
light exploded into the night. Chaos turned on itself. Victory
unfolded through obedience that defied logic.

That's how God still moves—through small, trembling yeses that ignite wildfires of deliverance.

Maybe this is your moment.

You feel small.
You feel outnumbered.

But God is whispering your name in the same cadence He spoke to Gideon:

"The Lord is with you, mighty one."

He's calling you out of hiding—out of the mental winepress of fear, comparison, and limitation—into the open field where His fire falls.

He's not looking for perfection.
He's looking for availability.

You may think you're threshing wheat in secret, but Heaven sees the spark in your hand.

It's ready to burn.

The same Presence that found Gideon is finding you now—not to shame your hiding, but to ignite your calling.

Soon, the fear that chased you will flee from the fire that burns within you.

That's the transformation of a renewed mind—when hiding hearts become holy fire, when survivors become revivalists.

So ask yourself:

What if this hiding place isn't your defeat, but your preparation?
What if God has been waiting for this moment to rename you?

The torch is already in your hand.

You were never meant to live in the shadows.

The voice that called Gideon is still echoing through generations—calling you by name.

Rise, mighty one.
Your winepress has become an altar.
And the fire that falls there will light the nations.

Jesus in the Wilderness: Wielding the Sword of Truth

After the fire falls in your spirit, the wilderness will come.

Not as punishment—but as proof.

Even Jesus, freshly baptized and affirmed by the Father's voice— *"This is My beloved Son, in whom I am well pleased"* (Matthew 3:17)—was immediately led by the Spirit into the wilderness to be tested.

Did you catch that? Led by the Spirit.

Not by Satan, not by sin—by the Spirit.

Because every true son or daughter must face the proving ground of identity. The wilderness is not where God abandons you; it's where He anchors you. It's where the whisper of the Father must grow louder than the lies of the enemy. For forty days, Jesus fasted. Forty days of silence, hunger, and heat.

And when His body was weakest, the enemy came—just like he came to Eve in Eden, just like he whispered to Gideon in hiding. He doesn't change his tactics; he only changes his tone.

And the first words out of his mouth were the same words he's still using on you today: *"If you are the Son of God..."* (Matthew 4:3)

That's always the heart of the attack—identity. The enemy will question what the Father already declared. He'll twist the Word to make you doubt who you are. Because if he can distort your identity, he can derail your destiny. But Jesus didn't engage the debate. He didn't reason. He didn't negotiate. He drew the sword.

"It is written…" (Matthew 4:4)

Three times the enemy came. Three times Jesus answered with the Word. No speculation. No fear. No panic. Just precision—truth spoken in power. That's not just a story—it's a strategy. Every lie that comes against your mind must be answered, not with emotion, but with Scripture.

When fear says, You're alone, you declare, *"He will never leave me nor forsake me"* (Hebrews 13:5).

When shame says, You've gone too far, you declare, *"There is therefore now no condemnation for those who are in Christ Jesus"* (Romans 8:1).

When despair says, This will never change, you declare, *"He who began a good work in me will bring it to completion"* (Philippians 1:6).

Truth is your weapon.

The Word of God is not paper and ink—it's a living sword forged in Heaven, breathed by the Spirit, and sharpened through obedience. When you speak it in faith, it cuts through darkness. When you declare it aloud, it dismantles the enemy's arguments brick by brick. Jesus didn't just quote Scripture; He embodied it.

He became the Word made flesh (John 1:14).

That's what you're called to—more than memorizing verses, you're invited to become what you believe. To let truth so saturate your thoughts that the enemy finds no foothold left.

Notice how the wilderness ended: *"Then the devil left Him, and angels came and ministered to Him"* (Matthew 4:11).

Every wilderness ends in visitation. Every test, when met with truth, leads to greater authority. When Jesus left the wilderness, He didn't leave wounded—He left armed.

Luke says, *"Jesus returned in the power of the Spirit"* (Luke 4:14).

Do you see it?

The wilderness that tried to break Him became the birthplace of His ministry. The same Spirit who led Him in now led Him out—with power. Maybe that's what your wilderness is doing too. What if the place that feels barren is actually the training ground for authority? What if the hunger, the silence, the testing aren't signs of God's absence but His preparation?

The Word you speak there—the truth you cling to when everything shakes—becomes the sword you'll wield for others later. Jesus didn't just survive the wilderness. He sanctified it. He turned it into holy ground for anyone who'd ever face the war in their thoughts. And He left us a pattern: Speak the Word. Stand your ground. Don't bow to the lie.

This is how we win the battle of the mind. Not by trying harder, but by yielding deeper. Not by fighting in the flesh, but by agreeing with truth until it becomes the air we breathe. Because every wilderness ends the same way—with a devil defeated and a son or daughter crowned with authority. And when you emerge, the very place that once tested you will tremble at the sound of your voice.

So if you're standing in the heat of your wilderness right now—don't despise it. Draw your sword. Speak what's written. Because you're not just fighting for your peace— you're training for your purpose. And soon, when the enemy flees, the same angels that ministered to Jesus will strengthen you for the next assignment. The wilderness isn't your ending; it's your awakening. It's the proof that you belong to the Kingdom above the sun. And when you step out, radiant and refined, the world will know—the Word works.

The War We're in Today

The wilderness never really ended—it only changed landscapes.

What once looked like deserts and serpents now glows in pixels and screens. The same enemy who whispered in Eden and tempted Jesus in the wilderness now hides in algorithms, headlines, and digital scrolls.

The stage has changed, but the strategy has not: **deception**.

We're living in a generation where distraction has become a form of bondage—where silence feels awkward and stillness feels like death. Identity is outsourced to likes and follows, and truth is decided by consensus instead of conviction.

This is not just cultural confusion; it's spiritual warfare disguised as entertainment.

The battle for truth is now fought in timelines and newsfeeds. Every scroll preaches. Some sermons lead to faith; others to fear.

The modern wilderness is not barren—it's noisy.

And the serpent still hisses, *"Did God really say?"*

Only now it comes through influencers, soundbites, and political outrage. It's subtle, it's constant, and it's shaping minds before they even realize they're in a fight.

Paul saw this day coming when he wrote:

"In the last days there will come times of difficulty. For people will be lovers of self, lovers of money, proud, arrogant, abusive... lovers of pleasure rather than lovers of God, having the appearance of godliness, but denying its power." (2 Timothy 3:1–5)

Does that not sound like the world around us?

We glorify self-expression while denying truth.
We chase affirmation while starving for belonging.
We scroll for purpose while ignoring Presence.

The deception is brilliant because it feels empowering while it's enslaving.

And yet—even in this—the Spirit of God is moving. Quietly. Fiercely. Relentlessly.

He's reclaiming the ground of the mind brick by brick, lie by lie. He's raising a people who don't just consume truth—they **carry** it. Men and women who can look straight into a sea of confusion and speak peace. Sons and daughters who no longer react to darkness but release light.

Make no mistake: this is a war for **agreement**.

If the enemy can win your focus, he can influence your faith. If he can occupy your thoughts, he can mute your authority.

But if your mind is renewed—if truth governs your inner world—your words will shake nations.

The rise in anxiety, depression, and identity crisis is not random; it's fallout.

When truth is dethroned, torment takes its place. When love is redefined without God, intimacy becomes idolatry. When feelings are exalted above Scripture, peace evaporates.

But when we return to His Word—when we wield the sword of truth in a generation drunk on deception—the fog lifts and light breaks through.

Think about it.

An entire generation has been discipled by the internet—its worldview shaped by feeds instead of faith, by screens instead of Scripture.

But the remnant rising now—the ones learning to think *above the sun*—are being discipled by the Holy Spirit Himself.

Their algorithms are heaven's rhythm: worship, prayer, truth, renewal. Their feeds are filled with testimony and prophetic fire. Their voices carry hope into the confusion of culture.

This is why the war for the mind matters.

It's not just about mental health—it's about spiritual authority. The enemy fears a believer who knows who they are and **Whose** they are.

Because once your thoughts are aligned with truth, you become unstoppable.

Jesus said, *"You will know the truth, and the truth will set you free."* (John 8:32)

But the opposite is also true. When lies rule your thoughts, bondage becomes normal.

That's why the renewal of the mind isn't optional—it's survival.

You cannot live above the sun while feeding on the dust of deception.

In these days, the Holy Spirit is calling for a new kind of warrior—not one armed with outrage or argument, but with discernment, peace, and the Word.

People who know when to speak and when to be silent. People who carry stillness in the storm. People who can stand in the center of digital chaos and emanate heaven's calm.

And I believe this is what we're seeing now.

A quiet revolution—not of noise, but of clarity.
Not louder—but clearer.
Not trendy—but true.
Not viral—but eternal.

Students shutting off their phones to pray.
Parents declaring truth over their homes.
Pastors preaching repentance instead of relevance.
Communities turning off the world's feed to tune into heaven's frequency.

This is revival in the age of information.

The serpent is still whispering.

But this time, there's a remnant who recognize the hiss, raise the sword, and reply:

"It is written."

And when they do, entire systems tremble.

Because no algorithm, no empire, and no deception can stand against the Word of the living God spoken in faith by a renewed mind.

The war for truth is fierce—but the victory is already secured.

You don't fight **to** win. You fight **from** the victory Jesus already won in the wilderness and on the cross.

So lift your head. Guard your gates. Renew your thoughts.

The same Spirit who led Jesus through the desert is leading you now—teaching you to wield truth in a world drowning in lies.

And when you walk above the sun, you won't just survive the war for your mind—you'll set captives free.

Breaking Agreement, Brick by Brick

How to dismantle lies and rebuild your inner world with truth

We've named the war. Now we get personal. Strongholds don't fall by accident; they fall by **intentional agreement with truth**. Think of this like stepping into a workshop with the Spirit—no shame, no hurry, just holy clarity.

Here's a clear, prophetic-practical path to tear down what hell built and raise a house of truth above the sun.

1) Get still and invite the Light

Slow your breathing. Put the phone face-down. Whisper, *"Holy Spirit, search me."* (Psalm 139:23–24; Psalm 46:10) Stillness is not empty; it's an altar where God speaks.

2) Name the lie

Write it in one sentence. Be specific.

- "I'm alone."

- "I am what I achieve."

- "God is disappointed in me." Lies lose power when they're dragged into light (Ephesians 5:13).

3) Expose the fruit

Ask: *What does this lie produce in me?* Fear, envy, isolation, rage, numbness? (Matthew 7:16–17; James 3:14–16)

Rotten fruit reveals a rotten root.

4) Renounce your agreement

Say it out loud:

"In Jesus' name, I renounce the lie that _________. I break agreement with it and reject its influence over my life." (2 Corinthians 4:2; 2 Corinthians 10:5)

5) Replace it with Scripture (the "It is written" exchange)

Find one verse that contradicts the lie and **say it aloud**. (Matthew 4:4,7,10)

- Lie: "I'm alone." → Truth: *"He will never leave you nor forsake you."* (Hebrews 13:5)

- Lie: "I am what I achieve." → Truth: *"You are God's workmanship."* (Ephesians 2:10)

- Lie: "God is disappointed in me." → Truth: *"He rejoices over you with singing."* (Zephaniah 3:17)

6) Declare, then personalize

Turn the verse into a declaration. (Romans 10:10)

- *"Abba, You are with me and for me. I do not walk alone."*

- *"I am crafted by God for good works He prepared."*

- *"Your song over me is louder than my shame."*

7) Envision from above the sun

Close your eyes and **picture** the truth playing out in your life (Colossians 3:1–2). See yourself walking into that meeting with peace. See your home lit with worship instead of worry. Sanctified imagination is not pretending; it's partnering.

8) Build a "truth card"

Write the lie (crossed out), the verse, and your declaration. Keep it in your pocket or Notes app. Review morning/noon/night. (Joshua 1:8)

9) Rewire with rhythm (renewal is repetition)

Truth must be rehearsed until it becomes your reflex.

- **Morning:** 5 minutes Scripture aloud + 2 minutes silence.

- **Midday:** One declaration + one grateful sentence.

- **Evening:** Brief examen—Where did I agree with truth? Where did I slip? (1 Thessalonians 5:17; Philippians 4:8)

10) Guard the gates you just cleared

Ask of every input: *Does this bring light or darkness?* (Proverbs 4:23)

- Unfollow chaos.

- Mute accounts that stir envy/fear.

- Set a **scroll curfew** (e.g., no screens the first/last 30 minutes   of   day). This is love for His presence, not legalism.

11) Use the 90-second reset when a lie hits hard

1. Breathe (4 counts in, 4 hold, 6 out).

2. Say: "It is written…" and speak your verse.

3. Worship one chorus for 60 seconds. Lies suffocate in praise (Acts 16:25–26).

12) Fast strategically

Choose a 24-hour media fast or one meal—pair it with Scripture and a short walk. Fasting clears static so truth comes through clean (Isaiah 58:6; Matthew 6:16–18).

13) Bring trusted community into the light

Confess the pattern; ask for prayer. (James 5:16) Agreement in truth multiplies freedom.

14) Establish a Truth Toolkit (carry these for quick draw)

By theme—pick one for your current battle:

- **Identity:** John 1:12; 1 Peter 2:9

- **Fear/Anxiety:** Isaiah 41:10; Philippians 4:6–7; Isaiah 26:3

- **Shame/Condemnation:** Romans 8:1; Psalm 103:12

- **Provision/Control:** Matthew 6:25–34; Philippians 4:19

- **Purity/Desire:** Psalm 119:9–11; 1 Thessalonians 4:3–5

- **Despair/Exhaustion:** Psalm 27:13–14; 2 Corinthians 4:16–18

15) Pray this "Agreement Prayer" daily for 30 days

"Jesus, I enthrone Your truth over my mind. I break agreement with every lie and submit my thoughts to Your Word. Let the meditation of my heart and the words of my mouth be pleasing to You (Psalm 19:14). Train me to answer every hiss with, 'It is written.' Amen."

A Sample Walk-Through (Try it now)

- **Trigger:** You sense, *"I'm falling behind; I'll never catch up."*

- **Name the lie:** Performance = worth.

- **Fruit:** Anxiety, hurry, envy, prayerlessness.

- **Renounce:** "In Jesus' name, I renounce the lie that my worth is my output."

- **Replace:** *"The Lord is my shepherd; I shall not want."* (Psalm 23:1)

- **Declare:** "You shepherd me; I lack nothing. Your pace is my peace."

- **Envision:** You working at a calm, faithful pace, joy present, no panic.

- **Rhythm:** Put Psalm 23:1 on your lock screen; pray it three times today.

- **Gate:** No email before Scripture tomorrow morning.

A 24-Hour Reset (when the swirl is thick)

1. **Morning (15 min):** Read Psalm 27 aloud. Write one lie → one verse.

2. **Midday (10 min):** Walk without phone; thank God for 3 specifics.

3. **Evening (15 min):** Worship one song; write a 3-line gratitude list; pray the Agreement Prayer.

Do this for one day. If peace returns, repeat tomorrow. Renewal is daily bread, not a single feast.

Remember the order

- **Expose** the lie.

- **Expel** the lie (renounce).

- **Exchange** it for truth (Scripture).

- **Exercise** the truth (practice).

This is how castles of confusion crumble and houses of wisdom rise. This is how you stop living under the sun's heaviness and start thinking from heaven's clarity. And as your inner world aligns, your outer world will follow—choices, relationships, assignments—all steadied by a mind set on things above.

Guarding the Gates of Your Mind

Building holy boundaries and keeping the river of peace flowing

You've just torn down the old walls—now comes the sacred task of building gates. Freedom isn't the absence of boundaries; it's the presence of the right ones.

Once the lies are exposed and expelled, the mind becomes new territory—a garden of peace that must be tended, guarded, and watered daily.

In Scripture, gates were never passive. They were places of authority, of watchmen, of decisions that shaped a city's destiny. The gatekeeper wasn't casual; he was vigilant, stationed at the threshold between safety and invasion. Your mind is no different. What you permit through your eye gates and ear gates determines what takes root in your heart. Proverbs 4:23 says, *"Above all else, guard your heart, for everything you do flows from it."*

The Principle of the Gate

Every gate is an invitation and a warning. Every song, show, post, or conversation carries an unseen sound wave—either heaven's harmony or hell's static. And your spirit is the tuner. You feel it, don't you? That subtle pull after scrolling too long, that heaviness after certain shows, that anxious swirl after news binges. That's not random—it's residue.

The kingdom of God operates on invitation, not intrusion. The enemy, however, works through *seduction*. He doesn't kick down your door; he slides through your feed, disguised as relevance. His whispers sound like normalcy: *"It's just entertainment." "It's just culture." "Everyone watches this."* But every unchecked allowance becomes an open gate.

Ask yourself this often:

Does this bring light or darkness?

Does this feed my spirit or drain it?

Do I feel peace or pressure after engaging?

Discernment begins with awareness. Peace is the Spirit's "green light"; disturbance is His "stop sign."

Eye Gates — What You Behold, You Become

Jesus said, *"The eye is the lamp of the body. So, if your eye is healthy, your whole body will be full of light"* (Matthew 6:22).

What you watch is shaping who you're becoming. Every glance, every frame carries power.

Entertainment isn't neutral—it disciples.

If a scene glorifies what Jesus died to save you from, it's not worth your gaze. If an image awakens envy, lust, or pride, it's not harmless; it's invasive. If the world mocks holiness, and you laugh along, you've let the enemy plant seeds in your soil.

You can't always control what flashes before you—but you can choose whether it stays.

David made a vow we'd do well to echo: *"I will set no worthless thing before my eyes"* (Psalm 101:3).

This isn't legalism—it's love. Love protects intimacy. Love says, *"I'd rather have His presence than my feed."* So, guard your eyes like you'd guard your covenant. Because what you behold, you become.

Ear Gates — The Sound That Shapes the Soul

Faith comes by hearing (Romans 10:17)—but so does fear. The voice you rehearse becomes the atmosphere you carry.

Music, podcasts, conversations—all are conduits of spirit. They either strengthen your peace or sabotage it.

Ask yourself: *Does this voice magnify truth or stir turmoil?*

You'll know by the residue it leaves. Some songs sound good but carry sorrow. Some podcasts seem intelligent but drip with cynicism. Some conversations feel friendly but leak gossip.

The enemy's favorite weapon isn't volume—it's familiarity. He wants his frequency to sound normal. But the more you fill your mind with worship, truth, and prayer, the quicker your spirit recognizes the counterfeit.

Cultivate a holy playlist for your soul—Scripture, worship, sermons that lift your gaze above the sun. Let what you hear prophesy peace into your day.

Soul Hygiene — The Rhythm of Renewal

Your mind is a garden, not a garbage can. You can't expect fruit if you never pull weeds.

That's why renewal requires rhythm. Here are practical watchman habits that keep the gates clean:

- **Firstfruits of Focus**: No phone before Scripture. Let God's voice be the first you hear.
- **Sabbath for Screens**: Once a week, silence notifications. Give your nervous system rest.
- **Midday Reset**: One worship song or Scripture declaration during lunch. Re-anchor peace.
- **Nightly Exchange**: Before sleep, hand God your worries. (Psalm 4:8)
- **Digital Tithing**: For every hour online, give God 10 minutes of prayer or reflection.

These aren't rules—they're rhythms of rest. They build margin around your mind so peace can flow like a river that never runs dry.

The Watchman's Posture

In Isaiah 62:6, God says, *"I have set watchmen on your walls; they shall never hold their peace day or night."* That's your call—to become a watchman of your own inner world.

Watchmen don't panic when they see shadows—they stand. They stay awake. They blow the trumpet when danger nears. The watchman's strength isn't fear—it's focus.

When anxiety tries to storm your gate, you don't crumble; you lift your shield.

When lust or bitterness knocks, you don't negotiate; you close the door and worship.

When despair whispers, you declare truth aloud until light breaks through.

The watchman's job is simple: keep the lamp burning.

A Holy Boundary Prayer

> *"Holy Spirit, make me a faithful gatekeeper. Let my eyes behold only what honors You. Let my ears discern Your voice above the noise. Teach me to say no to the serpent's subtleties and yes to Your still, small whisper. I choose peace over pressure, presence over performance, truth over noise. May the walls of my mind be salvation and my gates praise (Isaiah 60:18). In Jesus' name, amen."*

A Vision of a Guarded Generation

I see it—a generation walking through the world with clear eyes and unpolluted hearts. They scroll differently, speak differently, think differently. Their peace is loud; their purity contagious. While others are distracted, they are discerning. While others echo the noise, they carry the sound of stillness. Their phones become pulpits, their homes sanctuaries, their eyes full of light. They've learned that guarding their gates isn't retreat—it's warfare. And through their vigilance, the river of peace flows unbroken. That's the vision: a people who think above the sun, dwell in peace, and live as holy watchmen until the King returns.

A Renewed Mind in a Broken World

Look around—the world's unraveling at the seams, and much of the tearing starts in the mind.

Mental health is collapsing under the weight of unguarded thought life. Anxiety, depression, and confusion are no longer rare—they're epidemic. A generation that should be radiant with purpose is restless, burned out, and fractured. Young people chase identity through likes and viral trends, trying to capture significance in fifteen seconds of attention. Adults scroll to escape pain, hoping distraction will dull what only presence can heal.

Why is the soul so weary? Because when truth is sidelined, strongholds rise. When a culture trades revelation for reaction, peace disappears. The mind that was designed to host heaven becomes occupied territory. You see it everywhere—smiles fading behind filters, hearts silenced behind screens, lives lived outwardly connected but inwardly starving. But this isn't the end of the story.

There is a renewal breaking out across the earth—a quiet revolution of surrendered minds. Renewal often begins quietly, through small acts of obedience that realign the mind with heaven's rhythm. When distractions are laid down, when attention is returned to prayer, when presence is chosen over noise, something begins to heal. Joy reappears where it had thinned. Peace rises where anxiety once ruled. These simple decisions—made in hidden places—become doorways through which God restores clarity, affection, and spiritual vitality.

Paul's command still cuts through the noise like a trumpet blast: *"Take every thought captive to obey Christ"* (2 Corinthians 10:5).

Every thought will be captured by something—either by the world's scroll or by God's Word. One buries you under the sun; the other lifts you above it. The question isn't whether your mind will be shaped—it's by what. A renewed mind doesn't mean you never face fear again; it means fear no longer owns your focus. It doesn't mean you never battle lies; it means you now recognize their source.

Renewal is the recovery of sight—the ability to see life through the eyes of the Spirit instead of the lens of anxiety. It's peace that passes understanding not because life is quiet, but because the storm inside has bowed to a greater Voice.

The Spirit is breathing again on weary minds, washing away the static of the world, whispering, *"Come up higher. See as I see."*

When your thoughts are lifted above the sun, confusion gives way to clarity, striving gives way to surrender, and despair bows to divine perspective.

This is what it means to live renewed in a broken world—to become a sign and wonder of peace in an age of panic, a steady mind in a shaking culture, a voice of truth in a generation that's forgotten how to think for itself.

And this is the call before us now: to let truth shape what the world has distorted, to become walking sanctuaries of peace in a culture of noise. Because renewal isn't found in escape— it's found in encounter. The Word made flesh is still renewing minds today, one surrendered thought at a time.

The Prophetic Call to Rise

There's a holy urgency in the air—a sound cutting through the static of distraction and the noise of culture. It's the whisper of Holy Spirit calling His people to rise. Not to survive the shaking, but to shine in it. Not to hide from the darkness, but to carry light into it. This is the hour of divine recalibration.

The battle for your mind is not about mental wellness alone— it's about dominion. Whoever governs your thoughts, governs your future. And the Father is speaking even now: *"Come up higher. Think with Me. See from My throne. I am giving you the mind of Christ for the days ahead."* But the invitation comes with a cost.

You can't live above the sun while feeding on the world's shadows. You can't walk in authority while agreeing with lies. You can't carry glory while craving the approval of men.

Heaven's perspective requires a holy exchange—your thoughts for His, your will for His Word, your worries for His wisdom.

This is not theory. It's survival. It's holiness. It's destiny. A mind renewed by truth becomes a fortress the enemy cannot breach. A mind surrendered to Christ becomes a conduit for heaven's strategy on earth. Every surrendered thought is reclaimed territory. Every renewed imagination becomes a gateway for glory.

Listen to The Spirit saying: *"I am raising up a people who will think My thoughts and speak My words. They will stand in the chaos without fear, for their peace will not be borrowed—it will be born. Their minds will be sanctuaries of revelation, their words will carry creative power, and their discernment will pierce deception because they have learned to think above the sun."*

This is your call to rise—to guard your gates, to silence every whisper that contradicts His voice, to fix your thoughts on what is pure, noble, true, and praiseworthy until heaven's peace floods your mind.

This is not the season to shrink back—it's the season to set your mind like flint. Because the mind you renew today will shape the destiny you walk in tomorrow. And the Church that renews her mind will become the Bride who cannot be deceived. Lift your thoughts. Lift your gaze. Lift your life above the sun.

You were never meant to think like the world. You were meant to carry the mind of Christ—radiant, steadfast, and unshaken. So rise. Take every thought captive. Let His truth be your atmosphere and His peace your proof.

The King is coming—and He's calling you to think like heaven before you see it with your eyes.

A Vision of Minds Set Free

I see a generation rising—eyes clear, hearts steady, minds no longer dulled by noise but burning with Scripture's fire. They carry peace into chaos, truth into confusion, and the mind of Christ into every room they enter.

- Students praying Psalm 23 in dorm rooms, breaking free from comparison.

- Parents declaring truth at their tables, restoring fractured homes.

- Pastors preaching with courage, shattering strongholds of fear and shame.

Their thoughts aren't cluttered with the world's noise—they're filled with the fire of the Spirit, igniting revival wherever they go.

And now the invitation comes to you: break agreement with lies, cast down arguments, and let your mind be reshaped by His Word.

This is your moment to rise above the sun—to live, think, and move with the mind of Christ.

Your eyes are gates. Your thoughts are gates. What you behold, you become. And what you focus on, you make room for.

That's why, in the very next chapter, we'll step into the **law of beholding**—because what you gaze upon doesn't just shape your thoughts; it shapes your destiny.

Chapter 3 — What You Behold, You Become

Come on, friend—let's sit by the fire, heart to heart, and wrestle with a promise about your gaze that could change how you see everything.

The world is fighting for your eyes—screens glowing in your hands, headlines screaming from your phone, distractions pulling at every turn.

But your gaze shapes your soul, building on the mental battle we faced in Chapter 2.

Paul unveils the secret in 2 Corinthians 3:18: *"And we all, with unveiled face, beholding the glory of the Lord, are being transformed into the same image from one degree of glory to another. For this comes from the Lord who is Holy Spirit."*

Transformation doesn't start with grinding through willpower or checklists—it's about what you behold. Fix your eyes on Jesus and you become like Him. What you look at, you become—and in this hour, that truth is your lifeline to rise above the sun.

The Law of Beholding: A Spiritual Fire

There's a spiritual law etched into creation: what you behold, you become. What you focus on, you make room for. And what you fear, you empower. I've preached this for years—it's the heartbeat of my first book; *Set Your Mind on Things Above the Sun*—but in this hour Holy Spirit is emphasizing the language of beholding: guarding your eye gates, lifting your gaze. Focus magnifies. Focus multiplies. Focus defines your reality. Like sunlight through a magnifying glass—scattered, it only warms; focused, it ignites. Scattered attention brings little change; a steady gaze unleashes power.

Stare at fear and it seeps into your bones. Linger on bitterness and your heart hardens. Dwell on idols and they chain you. But fix your eyes on Jesus and His freedom, peace, and radiance begin to mark you, "from one degree of glory to another." I've felt it—hours lost to newsfeeds left me anxious; hours in worship, gazing at His Word, left me steady and alive with hope. Your gaze empowers what it rests on.

In our current environment, the world is a visual battlefield—reels, stories, ads, all engineered to hijack your eyes. It's not random; it's formation. But Holy Spirit calls you higher: behold Him, see as heaven sees, and carry His glory. This isn't willpower; it's worship—letting Holy Spirit do the heavy lifting as you lock eyes with Jesus.

Every human heart was designed with this built-in miracle. We are mirrors. Whatever we fix our eyes upon imprints itself on us. Paul unveiled it in 2 Corinthians 3:18: *"And we all, with unveiled face, beholding the glory of the Lord, are being transformed into the same image from one degree of glory to another. For this comes from the Lord who is the Spirit."*

Transformation does not begin with striving, but with seeing. The direction of your gaze determines the direction of your life. Beholding is not passive; it is participatory. The more steadily you look, the more deeply you are changed.

There is a spiritual physics to focus:

- What you focus on, you make room for.
- What you magnify, you empower.
- What you fear, you invite to rule.

Scattered attention warms you briefly but changes nothing; focused attention ignites you. Like sunlight through a lens, focus gathers energy until it becomes fire. That is why the enemy fights so fiercely for your eyes. He knows that whoever holds your gaze will soon shape your soul.

Look long enough at fear, and it seeps into your bones. Stare at bitterness, and it calcifies your heart. But behold Jesus—the radiance of the Father—and His light begins to re-form you from the inside out. His peace displaces anxiety; His purity rewrites desire; His presence becomes your atmosphere.

The Spirit is teaching the Church again that beholding is warfare. In a culture of distraction, attention is devotion. To behold Jesus is to defy Babylon's programming; it is to choose intimacy over information, adoration over opinion. Every moment you lift your eyes above the sun and fix them on the King, you participate in your own transfiguration.

This is not self-help. It is surrender.

It is not positive thinking. It is prophetic alignment—allowing your eyes to agree with heaven.

You were created to gaze, and that gaze was meant for God. When you behold Him, you begin to bear His likeness, *"from glory to glory."*

So pause here. Let your vision recalibrate. Breathe. Let the world's images fall away. The fire you carry tomorrow will be determined by what you behold today.

David's Gaze: Triumph and Tragedy

Let's walk softly onto the rooftop of Jerusalem. The night air is warm; the lamps flicker in the courtyards below. The kingdom rests, but its king does not. David—warrior, poet, worshiper—paces the stones of his palace roof, restless in the season when kings go to war. His eyes drift, and in that unguarded moment he beholds her—Bathsheba, bathing by the moonlight.

It starts with a glance.

A moment unsurrendered.

A heartbeat of curiosity that becomes captivity.

He could have turned away, but he lingered. And that lingering gaze unlocked a chain reaction—desire conceived sin, and sin gave birth to death. The spiral that followed—adultery, deceit, murder—didn't begin in the act; it began in the eyes.

This is the law of beholding written in human tragedy: what you stare at, you start to mirror. The eyes are architects of destiny. They build what the heart will later inhabit.

The rooftop was not David's first battlefield. Long before he faced temptation, he faced a giant. In the Valley of Elah, when the armies of Israel trembled, David's gaze lifted higher. He looked not at the towering frame of Goliath but at the unshakable covenant of Yahweh.

"The Lord who delivered me from the paw of the lion and the bear will deliver me from this Philistine." (1 Samuel 17:37)

His eyes that day were anchored in faith, and that gaze transformed fear into holy defiance. One look at God's greatness made the giant small. That same gaze that birthed courage on the battlefield, when left unguarded on the rooftop, birthed compromise in the heart.

Two stories—one man—two directions of vision. One beholden to glory, one captured by shadow.

The Spirit whispers through David's story: *your eyes are prophetic instruments.* They declare where your allegiance truly lies. Fix them on fear, and you empower it. Fix them on desire, and it rules you. Fix them on Jesus, and His likeness begins to imprint upon your soul.

When the prophet Nathan confronted David, conviction struck like lightning, but mercy followed just as swiftly. His restoration began where his fall began—with his sight. He turned his gaze from the ashes of failure to the mercy of God and cried,

"Create in me a clean heart, O God, and renew a right spirit within me." (Psalm 51:10)

That prayer was more than repentance; it was recalibration.

The Hebrew word *bara'*— "create"— is the same word used in Genesis 1: *"God created the heavens and the earth."* David wasn't asking for moral improvement; he was asking for new creation. He had learned that only divine light could restore what misplaced sight had darkened.

Pause and consider: how many of the battles we call "temptation" are really wars of vision? The rooftop wasn't the problem; the direction of the gaze was. What you continually behold, you eventually pursue. What you magnify, you move toward.

Look again at David's arc: when his eyes lifted heavenward, giants fell and kingdoms advanced; when his eyes fixated earthward, everything crumbled. The difference wasn't his calling, gifting, or anointing—it was his focus.

In these days, the same war for vision rages across every screen, billboard, and glowing feed. We are not merely fighting temptation; we are fighting formation. The world no longer asks for your allegiance outright—it simply asks for your attention, knowing that what captures your eyes will soon capture your heart.

So the Spirit asks you now:

Where are your eyes resting?

What are you beholding when no one is watching?

Because the trajectory of your gaze will determine the testimony of your life.

There's mercy for misdirected vision. David's story doesn't end with ruin but with restoration. The same God who met him in failure will meet you in focus. If you will lift your eyes again—away from the rooftop, away from the noise, away from the glittering idols of this age—and fix them on the beauty of the Lord, your story can shift from tragedy to triumph.

The rooftop still speaks.

Every generation must decide what it will behold when the night is quiet and the soul is restless. Will you linger on shadows or lift your gaze to glory? Because every eye lifted to Heaven becomes a mirror of its light. And the world, starved for radiance, is waiting to see that light reflected in you.

Moses: Beholding Glory, Shining Bright

Let's climb the mountain now.

Not the rooftop of temptation, but the summit of revelation. The air thins as we ascend, and the noise of earth falls away beneath us. The rocks crackle with the residue of holiness, and the air hums with presence. Moses stands before the blazing mystery of God—flame that does not consume, fire that does not destroy.

He has seen the miracles in Egypt, the plagues, the sea split like silk before the wind. But here on Sinai, he asks for something more. He doesn't ask for power or provision—he asks for Presence:

"Show me Your glory." (Exodus 33:18)

That one request changes everything.

It's the cry that separates leaders from lovers.

Moses wasn't content to see God's works; he wanted to see His face. He wanted the glory, not the glitter.

The Father answers not with denial, but with invitation. He hides Moses in the cleft of a rock and lets His goodness pass by. The mountain trembles. Light and cloud kiss. Heaven bends low to meet a man's hunger. And when Moses descends, something has shifted.

The people see it before he does—his face is radiant, glowing with unborrowed light (Exodus 34:29).

The residue of glory clings to him. He doesn't know it yet, but he has become what he beheld. That's the mystery of beholding: proximity changes countenance. You cannot stare at light and remain dim. You cannot dwell in glory and stay ordinary.

When Moses beheld God, he became a mirror of His radiance. The transformation was so tangible that the Israelites could not look directly at him. He veiled his face, not because the glory faded, but because the people feared the light that exposed their darkness. That veil, Paul tells us in 2 Corinthians 3, still blinds hearts that resist the Spirit. But *when one turns to the Lord, the veil is removed."* (v.16) Then we, like Moses, *"behold the glory of the Lord"* and are *"transformed into the same image from glory to glory."*

The invitation that once belonged to one man now belongs to every son and daughter washed in the Lamb's blood. Beholding is the pathway to transformation. It's not striving. It's not perfectionism. It's proximity. The glory you reflect tomorrow will depend on the Presence you pursue today.

Consider the contrast between David's rooftop and Moses' mountain. David lingered where his eyes were unguarded and fell into shadow.

Moses lingered where his eyes were unveiled and became light.

Both moments reveal the same law: *what you behold, you become.*

One man's gaze birthed compromise; the other's birthed communion.

Moses didn't come down from Sinai with a better strategy for leadership.

He came down with the Presence itself—his countenance a testimony that encounters change more than education ever can.

That is the Church's call in this hour—not to impress the world with intellect or structure, but to reflect the light of the One we've seen. The greatest apologetic is radiance.

You can tell when someone has been with Him. Their voice carries weight. Their eyes carry peace. Their life hums with quiet authority. That's the mark of those who have seen the King. They walk into rooms and darkness begins to retreat without a word. It's not charisma; it's communion.

This is the mountain invitation for our generation. While the world chases platforms and applause, heaven is still whispering the same question it asked Moses: *Will you come up higher?*

Not for blessing.
Not for favor.

Not for recognition.

But for Me.

In these days, when the Church often mirrors the world more than it mirrors Christ, the Spirit is calling us back to the mountain. The fire still burns. The invitation still stands.

And for those who say yes—for those who linger in His glory until their faces shine—the world will see again what it means to behold and become. You were made for radiant living. Not the flickering light of human success, but the steady glow of divine encounter. So lift your gaze, like Moses. Step into the cleft of the Rock—Christ Himself. Let His goodness pass before you. Let His fire mark you.

And when you come down from the mountain, don't rush to hide the light. The world needs to see it. Because in a generation drowning in darkness, the ones who've seen His face will become the mirrors that light the way home.

Peter: Eyes on Jesus or the Waves

Let's leave the mountain now and step into the storm.

The wind is fierce, the night thick with uncertainty. The disciples are straining at the oars, their faith flickering like the lantern at the bow. And suddenly—there He is.

Jesus.

Walking on the very waves that threatened to drown them.

The scene is both impossible and prophetic: the Creator treading upon chaos, the Word mastering the waters that once covered the deep. The storm is raging, but He is unmoved. The elements obey the One they remember.

Peter squints through the wind and calls out,

"Lord, if it is You, bid me come to You on the water." (Matthew 14:28)

And Jesus simply says, *"Come."*

That single word still echoes through every heart that dares to believe: Come.

Not after the storm passes. Not once the sea calms.

Come—while the waves still rise and the wind still screams.

Peter steps out, and for a moment, he lives what most only dream: walking above what others fear. He defies logic because his gaze is locked on the impossible made visible—Jesus. That's what faith looks like. It's not denial of the storm; it's focus in the midst of it.

But then, Scripture says, *"when he saw the wind,"* he began to sink. (Matthew 14:30)

Nothing changed but his focus. The same storm. The same sea. The same Savior. Only his gaze shifted—from the face of the Master to the movement of the waves.

That's the law of beholding again—what you look at, you move toward.

The moment Peter beheld the storm, he began to mirror it—chaotic, unstable, sinking fast. But when his eyes were on Jesus, he mirrored His steadiness, His dominion over the deep.

This is not a story about failure; it's a mirror of mercy.

Because as Peter sinks, Jesus immediately reaches out His hand and catches him. Not after a lecture. Not with delay. Instantly.

The same hand that sculpted the sea now lifts a trembling disciple back above it.

The whisper beneath the waves is still the same: Focus is formation.

Every time your eyes drift from His face to your fear, you begin to drown in what He already conquered. But when your eyes lock on His presence, the impossible becomes possible again.

Faith doesn't erase storms—it teaches you how to walk through them without losing sight.

You see, Peter's mistake wasn't stepping out; it was looking away.

The same principle governs every believer today. We start in fire, faith burning bright, but somewhere between the call and the completion, our gaze wavers.

We glance at the economy, the headlines, the opinions, the fears—and we start to sink under weights we were never meant to carry.

The war for your gaze is relentless because it determines your altitude. You can't rise while staring at the wind. You can't walk in peace while studying the storm. You can't carry glory while focusing on the chaos.

The enemy doesn't need to destroy your calling if he can distract your eyes. But there's mercy in the reach. Every time you sink, Jesus is near enough to lift you. His rebuke is gentle, almost tender: *"O you of little faith, why did you doubt?"*

It's not condemnation—it's invitation.

It's as if He's saying, *"You were doing it. You were walking above what once ruled you. You only forgot where to look."*

Peter would remember that moment for the rest of his life. Years later, when he stood before the Sanhedrin unafraid, or when he wrote to persecuted believers, urging them to fix their hope fully on the grace of Christ—he was speaking as one who had learned where to look.

He had learned that storms only drown those who stare at them. And perhaps that's where you are now—somewhere between the boat and the breakthrough. The waves are real. The wind is loud. Fear is whispering. But so is Jesus.

Come.

The waters that threaten to consume you are about to carry you—if you'll fix your gaze.

Lift your eyes again.

You were not called to survive the storm, but to reveal the One who walks upon it.

The Church in this hour must recover Peter's courage and Moses' gaze—the boldness to step out and the focus to keep looking up. Because faith that fixes its eyes on Jesus cannot drown.

The storm will pass, but what you behold in it will shape you forever.

And when you emerge—saturated but steadfast, trembling but transformed—you'll discover that the waves were never the test; the gaze was.

The War for Your Eyes in These Days

The war for your mind begins with your eyes.

The battle for your destiny begins with your gaze.

We are living in an age where attention has become the new altar—where whoever owns your focus owns your future. The enemy has learned that he doesn't need to steal your worship if he can scatter your gaze. Because once your eyes are divided, your heart soon follows.

The digital world has become the new Egypt, forming modern slaves with glowing chains. Scroll by scroll, image by image, it reshapes what we love, how we think, and even who we believe we are. This is not neutral. It's formation. It's worship disguised as entertainment.

Every scroll is a liturgy. Every click is a confession. Every gaze is a seed.

Our generation is being discipled by algorithms, not apostles. By screens, not Scripture. By endless entertainment that numbs the soul, not revelation that awakens it.

And behind it all, there is a spirit—a system—ancient and familiar: the same serpent that whispered to Eve in the garden, *"Did God really say?"* now whispers through pixels and platforms, *"Does truth really matter?"*

Pornography has become the new priest of this fallen temple, catechizing millions into shame. Lust is no longer hidden in alleys—it's algorithmically targeted, personalized, and delivered on demand.

The cost? Eyes darkened, hearts dulled, marriages eroded, souls fractured. Psalm 115:8 warns, *"Those who make idols become like them; so do all who trust in them."*

That is the invisible exchange: what you behold, you begin to mirror.

Outrage has become another idol—anger sold as virtue. Feeds filled with fury keep people addicted to offense, baptizing bitterness in the name of *"truth."* The more you stare at corruption, the more corrupted your peace becomes. The more you fixate on evil, the more its residue coats your soul. It's not apathy to look away—it's warfare.

Comparison is perhaps the quietest thief of all. It slips in while you scroll past someone else's highlight reel and whispers, "You're behind." But comparison is not conviction—it's counterfeit conviction. It pushes you to perform rather than to abide. It makes you measure your worth by moments that were never meant to define you.

The enemy's strategy hasn't changed since Eden; only the tools have evolved. He still aims for the eyes. Because he knows the eyes are the gates of glory—or the gateways of corruption. What you watch, you worship. What you feed on, you become.

Look at what's happening across culture. A generation once filled with promise is now drowning in confusion—gender distortion, moral inversion, spiritual amnesia.

They are not simply rebelling; they are reflecting what they've been beholding. Their identities are being rewritten by the images they consume. It's Babylon 2.0—beautiful, glittering, and deadly. But here's the truth the darkness cannot cancel: the same eyes that have been defiled can be sanctified again.

The same screens that once spread decay can become windows of awakening. The same attention that once served the serpent can now serve the King. Heaven is not retreating from this visual battlefield—it's invading it. Holy Spirit is anointing artists, filmmakers, worshippers, and intercessors who will release light into the digital highways. He's raising up a creative remnant who will not just react to culture but redefine it by what they behold.

The question remains: *What are you allowing to shape your sight?*

Because your gaze is your agreement. If you continually behold fear, you'll speak it. If you continually behold corruption, you'll carry it. If you continually behold Jesus, you'll radiate Him.

This is why Jesus said, *"The eye is the lamp of the body. So, if your eye is healthy, your whole body will be full of light."* (Matthew 6:22)

The enemy wants your lamp dimmed. But the Spirit is restoring vision—raising up a people who will guard their eyes not out of legalism but out of love.

To guard your gaze is not withdrawal—it's worship. It's saying, "My eyes are too sacred to feed the shadows."

If the world's images have trained you to crave noise, Holy Spirit will train you to love stillness.

If screens have conditioned you to scroll, He will teach you to see again—to look with wonder, with purity, with prophecy.

You'll start to see differently because you'll start to behold differently.

He is calling for a generation of Daniels who will not defile their eyes with Babylon's delicacies. He is calling for modern Moseses who will climb the mountain again. He is calling for sons and daughters who will make a covenant with their eyes, like Job, saying, *"I have made a covenant with my eyes; how then could I gaze at a virgin?"* (Job 31:1)

This covenant isn't about repression—it's about revelation. It's about protecting the glory that rests upon pure sight. Because the pure in heart will see God. (Matthew 5:8) The war for your eyes is not just moral—it's prophetic. The enemy wants to distort your vision so you can't discern what Heaven is doing. But when your eyes are clean, your discernment sharpens, your authority strengthens, and your peace deepens.

There is a remnant rising—eyes fixed like flint, gazes lifted above the noise. They don't bow to the god of distraction. They don't binge on darkness. They look upon the beauty of the Lord and reflect His light into the storm. You are being invited to join them. Lift your gaze. Guard your sight. Turn from the endless scroll of shadows and fix your focus on the face of Christ. Because what you behold in this hour will determine what you become in the next. The war for your eyes is the war for your destiny. And Heaven is calling you to see differently—until the light in your eyes becomes the light that guides a generation home.

Guarding Your Eye Gates: A Covenant of Love

Every revival begins with a decision of the eyes. Before a heart burns, the gaze must turn. Before a generation awakens, it must learn again where to look. Your eyes are not random; they are royal. They were created as gateways of glory—designed to behold the beauty of the Lord and reflect His light into the earth.

The fall did not erase that design; it only distorted its direction. And now, in these days of shaking and divine alignment, Holy Spirit is calling His people to reclaim their sight—to make a covenant of love with their eyes. Job understood this when he declared, *"I have made a covenant with my eyes; how then could I gaze at a virgin?"* (Job 31:1)

This wasn't legalism. It was longing.

Job wasn't afraid of looking—he was in love with holiness. He wasn't protecting himself from sin as much as he was protecting his intimacy with God. His eyes were too sacred to serve shadows.

That's the invitation before us now.

To move beyond rules into relationship. To see purity not as restriction but as protection of Presence. Because whatever captures your gaze will soon captivate your heart.

The eyes are gates—thresholds between the natural and the spiritual. Through them, truth enters or deception gains permission. Through them, peace flows in or anxiety takes root. Every glance carries spiritual weight. Every image you entertain builds or breaks a wall within your soul.

That's why Proverbs 4:25 commands, *"Let your eyes look directly forward, and your gaze be straight before you."*

It's not poetic—it's prophetic. The Spirit is teaching us that direction follows attention. The more we look at the world, the more we drift toward its gravity. The more we fix our gaze on Jesus, the more we are pulled into His orbit of peace and power.

So what does it mean to make a covenant with your eyes today? It's not about closing them—it's about consecrating them. It's learning to ask, "Does this bring light or darkness?" When a movie scene stirs lust, turn your eyes. When a post breeds envy, scroll past. When an image ignites anxiety, shut the gate. Not because you fear the world, but because you treasure His Presence.

Each decision to guard your gaze is an act of love, not deprivation. Each refusal to feed the flesh strengthens your spirit. Each moment you look away from shadows, your eyes are restored to see the King in His beauty (Isaiah 33:17). This is not about withdrawing from the world—it's about seeing it rightly.

The pure in heart see God everywhere—in the sunrise, in the laughter of a child, in the eyes of a stranger. The world doesn't lose its color when your eyes are consecrated; it becomes radiant with redemption.

Guarding your eyes is the discipline of the watchman. It's choosing vigilance over vanity, awareness over apathy. Watchmen don't close their eyes to darkness—they stay alert to protect what's holy. The Spirit is raising up such watchmen now—sons and daughters who know how to see without absorbing, to witness without worshipping what is not God. Their sight is sanctified. Their discernment sharp. Their focus anchored. They don't feed on the news for fear; they behold the throne for perspective. They don't gaze on scandal; they gaze on Scripture. They don't feast on distraction; they fix on devotion.

The devil has always wanted to blind the Church with the dust of distraction. But the breath of God is clearing vision again. He's washing eyes with the oil of intimacy. He's teaching His people to see through tears of repentance and behold through lenses of glory.

So, friend, make a covenant of love with your eyes—not as a vow of fear, but as an offering of devotion.

Say to Him in prayer: *"Lord, my eyes are Yours. I surrender what I see, how I see, and where I look. Make my vision clear. Let my gaze be steady. I want to behold what You behold, to love what You love, to turn away from what dims the light within me."*

Each time you honor that covenant, you'll feel His pleasure. Each time you lift your eyes from the noise to His face, peace will rush in like a river.

The presence you protect will become the glory you carry. Because when your eyes are pure, your whole body becomes light. And when your gaze is steadfast, your spirit becomes flame. Guard your eyes, not just for what they see, but for who they're becoming.

You were born to behold the King—and what you behold, you become.

The Subtle Thief: Distraction's Drain

Not every thief shouts. Some steal in silence. The most dangerous enemy of this generation's anointing is not persecution or poverty—it's distraction. It doesn't roar; it drips. It doesn't demand your faith; it just diverts your focus. And if the enemy can't make you sin, he'll simply make you busy. Distraction is the slow leak of destiny. It's the dull hum that keeps you scrolling when heaven is speaking. It's the subtle pull that turns your prayer time into performance and your worship into multitasking. It disguises itself as productivity, but it robs you of presence.

James wrote, *"A double-minded man is unstable in all his ways."* (James 1:8)

Double-mindedness isn't always disbelief—it's divided attention. It's trying to behold God while still feeding on noise. It's glancing at heaven but living in notifications. It's trying to climb the mountain while tethered to the world's chatter below. The danger of distraction is that it doesn't feel demonic—it feels normal. It doesn't crash your life; it clutters it. It doesn't destroy devotion in a day; it drains it by degrees.

You don't even notice the fire dimming until prayer feels heavy, worship feels mechanical, and silence feels awkward. That's how the subtle thief works. He doesn't need to convince you God isn't real—he just needs to keep you too busy to care.

In the days of Elijah, Jezebel couldn't outpower the prophet, so she tried to outshout him. But the Lord was not in the wind, or the earthquake, or the fire—He was in the whisper. (1 Kings 19:11–12)

That whisper still speaks, but only the undistracted can hear it.

Our age has inverted Elijah's moment—now, the noise is the culture, and the whisper is the call of God buried beneath it.

Every beep, buzz, and banner competes for your gaze. Every app is a golden calf for the modern mind, built to consume the time that once belonged to prayer.

Jesus warned of this danger in the parable of the sower:

"The cares of the world and the deceitfulness of riches choke the word, and it proves unfruitful." (Matthew 13:22)

The seed wasn't stolen—it was suffocated. That's distraction. It doesn't attack; it asphyxiates. The tragedy is that many are mistaking distraction for discernment. We think staying informed is being wise, but endless consumption only breeds confusion. We claim we're staying "connected," yet the more we scroll, the lonelier we become. We say we're "resting," but rest without communion is just numbness dressed as peace.

You can't fix your eyes on God and feed on noise without wobbling.

The spirit of distraction is the modern Jezebel—designed to exhaust prophets, to drain vision, to silence intercession. But there's an Elijah company rising who will not be baited by Babylon's noise. They are learning to turn off the volume of the world to tune into the whisper of the Spirit.

Here's the prophetic truth: You can't carry the weight of glory while juggling the weight of everything else.

You can't think above the sun while your thoughts orbit your inbox.

You can't host heaven's presence while constantly reacting to earth's notifications.

This isn't condemnation—it's correction born of love.

Holy Spirit is gently but firmly drawing a line: *"Choose what matters."*

There's a sacred stillness He's trying to reintroduce to His people—a rhythm of rest that restores clarity.

When you sit before Him in silence, without agenda or performance, the fog begins to lift. The noise of the world loses its grip, and you remember again what peace sounds like.

This is why Jesus often withdrew to lonely places to pray. (Luke 5:16) He didn't withdraw because He was weak—He withdrew to stay aligned. He left the crowd to stay close to the Father. If Jesus Himself needed undistracted communion, how much more do we?

You were not created for constant input; you were designed for divine intimacy. You were not built for endless scrolling; you were built for beholding. The more you fill your life with noise, the less capacity you have for glory. So here's the call: unplug to reawaken. Turn down the world's volume and let the Word speak again.

Fast not just from food, but from the flood of information that clogs your spirit. Take your eyes off the swirl and fix them back on His face. Distraction's drain stops the moment you pause and listen. Presence begins when performance ends. The flame rekindles when focus returns.

Heaven is looking for undistracted lovers—men and women who will turn aside like Moses before the burning bush, saying, *"I must see this great sight."* (Exodus 3:3)

Those who learn to look again will hear what others miss.

Friend, your deliverance from distraction won't come by discipline alone—it will come by desire. Fall in love with His presence again. Crave His voice above every other. Let adoration silence anxiety. Because what you give your attention to is what you worship. And what you worship is what you will become. So guard your gaze. Guard your time. Guard your heart. Don't let the subtle thief drain what the

Spirit is trying to fill. The next great move of God won't come through multitaskers—it will come through the focused.

Through those who dare to say, *"One thing have I desired of the Lord… to gaze upon His beauty."* (Psalm 27:4)

The world will call it unproductive. Heaven will call it revival.

Beholding in the Wilderness: Jesus' Example

Every son and daughter of God will walk through a wilderness. It's the proving ground of purity, the classroom of clarity, the forge where identity is refined by fire. The wilderness doesn't expose your weakness—it reveals your focus.

Jesus understood this.

Before the miracles, before the crowds, before the cross—there was the wilderness.

Led by the Spirit, not by sin, He was taken into the desert to face the enemy head-on (Matthew 4:1). It wasn't punishment—it was preparation. Heaven had declared over Him, *"This is My beloved Son, in whom I am well pleased."* The wilderness would test whether He would believe it.

Forty days. No food. No comfort. No distraction.

Only the Spirit, the silence, and the serpent.

The enemy came not with weapons, but with words. *"If You are the Son of God…"* (Matthew 4:3)

The same hiss that deceived Eve now slithered toward Jesus. But unlike Adam, Jesus did not entertain the lie. Unlike Israel, He did not bow to hunger, pride, or power. He fixed His gaze on the Father.

Three temptations—three moments of beholding.

- When hunger gnawed at His body, He beheld the Word: *"Man shall not live by bread alone, but by every word that comes from the mouth of God."* (Matthew 4:4)
- When pride whispered for spectacle, He beheld trust: *"You shall not put the Lord your God to the test."* (Matthew 4:7)
- When ambition offered kingdoms, He beheld worship: *"You shall worship the Lord your God, and Him only shall you serve."* (Matthew 4:10)

He wielded no sword but Scripture. He stood not in strength but in surrender. His eyes never left the Father. And when the devil fled, the angels came and ministered to Him.

That is the law of beholding in its purest form—focus under fire.

Jesus did not escape the wilderness; He endured it with His gaze intact.

The same Spirit who led Him there is leading His Church there again—not into desolation, but into discernment.

In a world where abundance has become anesthesia, the wilderness strips away the noise until only truth remains. It is the place where distractions die and devotion is reborn. We often pray, *"Lord, take me out of the wilderness,"* but the wilderness is where God takes the world out of us.

It is not a punishment—it's a purification.

It is where false appetites are starved, false identities are shattered, and false comforts are exposed for what they are. In that silence, the soul remembers its source. In that hunger, the heart rediscovers its satisfaction. In that stillness, the eyes refocus on glory.

Jesus left the wilderness *"in the power of the Spirit"* (Luke 4:14).

Notice that—He entered led by the Spirit but emerged empowered by the Spirit. What changed? His focus had been tested and proven true. That's what happens when you behold rightly in barren seasons. The fire doesn't destroy you—it refines your vision.

Temptation doesn't disqualify you—it clarifies your dependence.

Isolation doesn't waste you—it awakens you.

The enemy tempts you to look away; the Spirit trains you to look through. To see the unseen. To fix your eyes not on what is visible and temporary, but on what is eternal. (2 Corinthians 4:18) And if you listen closely, even in your wilderness, you'll hear the whisper that sustained the Son: *"You are still My beloved."* Because identity doesn't dissolve in deserts—it's deepened there.

The wilderness doesn't steal your vision—it sanctifies it. It teaches you to gaze at God when there's nothing else to see. Maybe you're there right now—alone, uncertain, feeling stripped of everything that used to steady you. Don't despise this season. Don't curse the silence. Lift your eyes. The wilderness is not abandonment; it's invitation.

When Jesus looked at the Father, the desert became holy ground. When you do the same, so will yours. You don't have to wait for the storm to pass or the provision to come. You can behold Him right here—in the heat, in the hunger, in the hidden place. Every wilderness becomes a window when your eyes are fixed on Him. That's the secret of true authority:

Before you can speak to storms, you must first learn to see through sand. Before you can cast out devils, you must first conquer distraction. Before you can lead revival, you must first master your gaze. The desert will end—but what you behold there will mark you for life.

When you emerge, you will walk in the power of the Spirit, not the exhaustion of effort. Your words will carry weight. Your presence will carry peace. Your eyes will carry light. And the world will know—you've seen something.

You've been somewhere. You've beheld Someone.

The Church's Mandate: Reflect His Glory

The wilderness purifies the gaze, but the purpose of that gaze is not survival—it's reflection. The call of the Church in this hour is not to compete with the world's light shows, but to radiate the uncreated light of God. We were never meant to mirror culture; we were meant to mirror Christ. *"You are the light of the world. A city set on a hill cannot be hidden."* (Matthew 5:14) Jesus didn't say, You will become the light. He said, *You are the light.*

Not a borrowed glow. Not a manufactured brand. You are carriers of glory because you were made in His image and filled with His Spirit.

But light only shines when the gaze is clear. The Church that looks too long at the world begins to dim like a candle trapped in smoke.

We've spent years trying to make the Church relevant, when she was *called to be radiant.*

Programs multiplied while prayer rooms emptied. Platforms grew taller while altars grew colder. We began reflecting opinions instead of Presence, algorithms instead of anointing. We traded fire for familiarity, glory for graphics.

But the Spirit of God is shaking His Bride awake. He's peeling back the veil of performance and calling her back to simplicity—the gaze.

This is the hour of refocusing, the hour of returning to first love. Relevance has run its course; only revelation will carry us now. The world doesn't need a better production—it needs a clearer reflection.

It's not excellence that transforms; it's encounter.

And encounter is born from beholding.

When Moses came down from Sinai, his face shone because he had seen God. (Exodus 34:29) He didn't try to glow. He didn't brand the experience. He carried what he had beheld.

That's what the Church must recover: not a message polished for applause, but a people marked by Presence.

When a congregation beholds together, cities shift. When worship becomes gazing instead of performing, heaven opens. When pulpits are filled with those who've been in the fire, not just studied it, revival breaks out. It's not charisma the world is longing for—it's clarity.

They want to see something real, someone who's been with Jesus.

Like the disciples in Acts 4:13—untrained, unpolished, but unmistakably radiant because they had been with Him.

That's what revival looks like. Not new songs, but new sight. Not hype, but holiness. Not numbers, but nearness.

The Church's mandate is not to outshine the world's brilliance, but to host a different kind of light—one that burns from within.

When we behold the Lamb, we reflect the Lion.

When we fix our eyes on His glory, His image is etched into our countenance.

When we gaze on His Word, we begin to walk as His Word made flesh in the earth. We are mirrors of His majesty. We are lanterns of His love. We are reflectors of His reign.

That's why the enemy wars so violently for the Church's focus. He doesn't need to destroy her—just distract her. Because a distracted Church is a dim Church. But a beholding Church is unstoppable.

In these days of shaking, God is raising communities where the Presence is the program and the Word is the wonder. Homes that have become altars. Living rooms that have become upper rooms. Hearts that burn more fiercely than any stage could ever hold. The Spirit is saying again, *"Arise, shine, for your light has come, and the glory of the Lord has risen upon you."* (Isaiah 60:1)

That's not a metaphor—it's a mandate. The glory of God is meant to rest on His people until nations take notice.

Until fear gives way to faith. Until darkness is pierced by devotion. Until the earth is filled with the knowledge of His glory as the waters cover the sea. (Habakkuk 2:14)

The world is not waiting for another sermon—it's waiting for a reflection. When the Bride mirrors the Bridegroom, the harvest will come running.

When the Church stops glancing at herself and starts gazing at Him, the Spirit will pour out like fire on dry wood.

Friend, this is your part in that story. You are not a spectator—you are a mirror. You are not a bystander—you are a bearer of glory. Every moment you lift your eyes, every time you choose the secret place over the spotlight, you polish the mirror of your soul.

The more clearly you behold Him, the more brightly you'll reflect Him. And that reflection is what hell fears most.

So rise, radiant one. Wash your eyes in the river of His Word. Fix your focus on the One whose eyes burn like fire. You don't need to try to shine—just look at Him. The light will take care of itself. Because the Church's greatest weapon has never been her strategy—it's her sight.

And when her eyes are fixed on the King, no darkness can dim her flame.

My Story: Finding Focus in the Noise

The world is loud, friend—so loud that silence now feels strange.

Everywhere you turn, something is demanding your attention. The scroll never ends. The feed never stops. The noise never sleeps. And yet, amid the constant hum, a quiet voice still whispers, *"Be still, and know that I am God."* (Psalm 46:10)

The war for your focus is the war for your fire. The enemy knows he doesn't need to destroy your faith if he can just divide your attention. He doesn't need to silence your worship if he can keep you scrolling long enough to dull your desire.

Distraction is not neutral—it's spiritual warfare disguised as convenience.

In this age of noise, focus has become holiness. Stillness has become warfare. And beholding has become resistance. The mind can only hold what the heart adores.

That's why Jesus said, *"Where your treasure is, there your heart will be also."* (Matthew 6:21)

Whatever you treasure, you'll look at.

Whatever you look at, you'll become like.

And whatever you become like, you'll reproduce in your world.

The question then isn't What are you hearing? It's *What are you beholding?* Because there's a vast difference between information and revelation. Information informs the mind, but revelation transforms the soul. Information keeps you busy; revelation keeps you burning. One fills your time; the other fills your heart.

Heaven is calling for a people who will look again—who will quiet the noise long enough to hear the whisper. The whisper that guided Elijah through despair. The whisper that steadied Peter through the storm. The whisper that sustained Jesus through the wilderness.

There is a holy rhythm available to you, even in this digital chaos—a cadence of clarity that cuts through confusion.

It begins when you stop trying to keep up with the world and start keeping pace with heaven. Turn your focus back to the One who never wavers. Shut the door, silence the noise, and say with David, *"One thing have I asked of the Lord, that will I seek after: to dwell in the house of the Lord all the days of my life, to gaze upon the beauty of the Lord and to inquire in His temple."* (Psalm 27:4)

That's not poetry—it's prophecy.

It's the way forward for a Church called to shine in a world gone dim. The truth is, focus doesn't come from trying harder—it comes from loving deeper. When you fall in love with His presence, distraction loses its pull. When you make room for His voice, the noise of the world fades to static. When you fix your gaze on the eternal, the temporary loses its grip. That's why beholding is not a task—it's a love affair. It's not about escaping the world; it's about engaging it through a higher lens. It's seeing every moment—every sunrise, every person, every battle—through the light of His glory.

Heaven is teaching the Church again to breathe—to remember what stillness sounds like, what awe feels like, what focus does to the soul.

For when your gaze is full of God, your heart becomes unshakable.

And in a generation addicted to noise, a single focused life becomes a beacon of peace. This is what it means to live above the sun: Not to ignore the chaos, but to rise above it. Not to escape the world, but to bring heaven's perspective into it. Not to fight the noise with more noise, but to release a sound born in stillness. You can't reflect what you refuse to behold. But once your eyes are locked on Him, your life becomes a mirror of His majesty. So slow down. Breathe again. Lift your eyes. The Shepherd is still speaking between the headlines. The King is still walking on the waters of this age. And those who fix their gaze will not sink—they will shine.

The Prophetic Call to Behold

There's a sound rising again in the Spirit — faint at first, like a distant rumble across the horizon — but growing louder, clearer, nearer.

It's the sound of a generation awakening.

The sound of hearts turning, eyes lifting, and spirits coming alive under the weight of His glory. Holy Spirit is calling His people to behold. This is not a gentle suggestion. It is a trumpet blast from heaven. *"Behold the Lamb of God, who takes away the sin of the world!"* (John 1:29)

That cry still echoes through time. Every revival, every awakening, every turning of hearts begins here — not in striving, not in strategy, but in a gaze.

Beholding is not passive observation. It's prophetic participation. To behold is to agree with heaven's vision, to anchor your attention where the world can't pull it away.

To behold is to say, *"I refuse to let my eyes define my reality. I will see as God sees."*

The enemy has filled the atmosphere with distraction because he fears a focused Bride. He trembles at a generation that will turn its eyes from idols and fix them on the King. He knows that what you behold, you become — and what you become, you will release.

When the Church begins to behold Jesus again — not as an idea but as a Person — cities will tremble under the weight of His presence.

Marriages will heal in the glow of His love.

Addictions will break under the light of His gaze.

Nations will shift as hearts are reoriented to His throne.

That's why the Spirit is crying out: "Look again." Look past the chaos. Look beyond the noise. Look above the sun. Lift your eyes from the dust of this age to the dominion of His glory. Lift your focus from fleeting news to the eternal Word. Lift your gaze from fear to faith — from confusion to clarity — from yourself to the Savior.

Every revival begins with a beholding people. Every transformation begins with an unveiled face. Every encounter begins with a lifted gaze. And the Spirit is asking even now: *"Where are those who will look long enough to burn?"* Because beholding births burning.

Those who behold Jesus cannot remain neutral; their hearts ignite. The more you look, the more you love. The more you love, the more you shine. And the more you shine, the more darkness loses its grip.

This is the invitation — not to do more, but to see more. To see Him rightly until everything else finds its place. To gaze until your thoughts shift, your words carry weight, and your life becomes a living reflection of His glory.

The Spirit is drawing the Bride out of distraction and back into devotion. He's saying, *"Behold Me again, and I will restore your wonder."* Behold Me, and I will heal your vision. Behold Me, and I will awaken your first love.

This is not just about revival — it's about revelation. Because you cannot reveal what you have not first beheld.

And the world is waiting for a revelation of Jesus through a people whose eyes are filled with Him. So lift your gaze. Lift your worship. Lift your life. Let the veil fall. Let the light in. Let your heart burn again.

For the Bride who learns to behold will carry a beauty this world cannot counterfeit — radiant, fearless, and full of fire. And as she looks into His eyes, she will hear the same words that sent Isaiah: *"Whom shall I send, and who will go for us?"* (Isaiah 6:8)

This is your call to rise — not by might, not by power, but by focus. The King is coming, and He's training His people to see before they shine.

He's calling His Church to live with unveiled faces, hearts fixed on glory, and eyes that never wander from His.

Behold Him — and become what you behold.

A Vision for Beholding Hearts

I can see it—a generation awakening, eyes clear and hearts steady, walking through the chaos of this world with faces that shine like the dawn.

They are not distracted; they are devoted. They are not consumed by fear; they are consumed by fire. They move through classrooms, workplaces, cities, and nations carrying the fragrance of heaven and the light of the Lamb. They are a beholding generation—those who have seen the King and cannot look away. They do not chase platforms; they carry presence. They do not seek applause; they seek His eyes.

Everywhere they go, atmospheres shift because they live from a greater reality—one gaze, one glory, one God. They have chosen the better portion, like Mary at His feet, and the world cannot take it from them.

I see students in dorm rooms kneeling on the floor, Bibles open, tears falling onto pages as the Word becomes life inside them.

I see fathers and mothers turning off their screens, gathering their children around the table to pray, the glow of His presence replacing the flicker of entertainment.

I see pastors stepping out of the pressure to perform and stepping into the presence that transforms, preaching not to impress but to reveal.

I see worshipers who sing without striving because they've already seen His face.

I see prophets who speak not from outrage but from intimacy, declaring truth with tears and tenderness.

I see churches whose ceilings cannot contain the sound of unity, where every heart beats in sync with heaven's rhythm: *"Holy, holy, holy is the Lord God Almighty."*

This is the vision—what heaven is writing even now: A generation whose eyes are pure, whose hearts are undivided, whose lives have become mirrors of majesty. They will not be swayed by politics, popularity, or pressure, because their focus has found its home in the eyes of Jesus. They will be radiant with peace in a time of panic, steady in storms, gentle in truth, bold in love. They will walk in the authority of the Lamb because they live under the gaze of the Lion.

This is what revival truly looks like—not just crowds in arenas, but hearts in communion. Not just noise and movement, but stillness and fire. A people who carry His likeness because they never stop looking at Him.

And it's already happening.

In quiet places, unseen rooms, forgotten corners—He is raising His reflectors. They are learning that the light of His countenance is better than the spotlight of men. They are being transformed from glory to glory, not by effort, but by encounter. Every lifted gaze becomes a doorway for the Spirit to move. Every surrendered focus becomes a spark for awakening.

The Spirit is whispering to this generation: *"You were born for My gaze. Lift your eyes, and I will lift your life. The more you behold Me, the more you will reveal Me."*

This is the fruit of a renewed mind and a single focus—a people whose attention is worship, whose sight is sanctified, whose lives have become a reflection of heaven's light. And when the world sees them—this beholding generation—they will not see perfection; they will see Presence.

They will see peace that makes no sense, love that never quits, and eyes that burn with eternity. This is the people of Psalm 24— *"The generation of those who seek Him, who seek Your face, O God of Jacob."*

They will ascend the hill of the Lord, stand in His holy place, and carry His glory down into the valleys. They will live above the sun and call others higher, until the earth is filled with the knowledge of His glory as the waters cover the sea.

That's the vision: a people who behold Him until the world sees Him through them.

A generation of beholders who become revealers. Hearts fixed. Eyes clear. Lives aflame. The King is coming soon. Let this be the generation that greets Him not with distraction, but with devotion. Not with noise, but with nearness. Not with fear, but with fire.

Lift your gaze.

Behold the Lamb.

And let your life become His reflection— shining above the sun until the world is lit with His glory.

For Today: A Prophetic Invitation to Behold

Pause here.
Breathe.
Let the rush of the day fall away for a moment.

Heaven is inviting you to lift your eyes.

The world has trained you to look down—to screens, to circumstance, to shadows—but the Spirit is calling you to look up.

Beholding is not a task; it's a turning.

It's the decision to redirect your gaze from what drains you to the One who defines you. And right now, the Father's voice is whispering: *"Lift your eyes. I want you to see Me again."*

This is where transformation begins—not in striving, but in seeing.

What you behold, you become.
What you magnify, you manifest.
What you stare at long enough begins to shape your heart.

So today, make this your covenant:

To guard your eyes like sacred gates.
To give your attention only to what carries light.
To fix your focus not on fear, but on faith.
To fill your gaze with Jesus until His reflection becomes your reality.

Here is your invitation—simple, but sacred:

Turn from shadows. Unfollow what dims your light, feeds fear, or fuels comparison.

Fix your gaze. Open His Word, pray Psalm 27:4, and linger in His presence until peace settles over you.

Guard your eyes. Fast from noise. Choose stillness. Protect your focus like the treasure it is.

Reflect His glory. Carry His presence into every space you enter, until others glimpse His light in your eyes.

Beholding is the beginning of becoming.

When you see Him, you start to shine like Him.
When you focus on His face, fear loses its hold.
When you behold His beauty, holiness no longer feels like effort—it feels like love.

So wherever you are—in a quiet room, a moving bus, or beneath a weary sky—lift your gaze. Let the noise fade. Let the light fill you.

And let this simple prayer rise from your heart:

Prayer of Beholding

Jesus, I turn my eyes to You.
Cleanse the lens of my heart from distraction and fear.
Let every shadow fade in the light of Your glory.

Teach me to see as You see—to love what You love, to desire what You desire.
Transform me from the inside out, from glory to glory, until I reflect Your face to the world.

I choose to live above the sun, with my eyes fixed on You.
Amen.

You were not made for the noise—you were made for His nearness.
You were not designed to chase light—you were designed to carry it.

Lift your gaze.
Behold the King.

And let your life shine as His reflection until the world sees His glory through you.

From Beholding to Enduring

Every transformation begins with a gaze—but every destiny is proven in a fire.

When you learn to behold the Lord's glory, His image begins to form within you. Yet that image must be refined, tested, and revealed through endurance. The mountain of beholding always leads to the valley of proving.

What you've seen in the secret place must be carried through betrayal, injustice, and delay until it shines with incorruptible light. The same eyes that behold His beauty must also learn to behold His faithfulness when the pit closes in.

This is where Joseph steps onto the stage—not as a distant figure in Genesis, but as a prophetic mirror for our generation. He shows us what happens when a beholding heart walks through fire without losing its gaze.

Because the One you behold in glory is the One who walks beside you in the dungeon. And the same presence that transfigures you in worship will sustain you in waiting.

So now, friend, draw close again.

Let's sit with Joseph—the dreamer who refused to let betrayal define him. Let's trace the presence of God through his pit, his prison, and his palace, and discover the anointing that will carry you through your own season of testing.

Chapter 4 — The Joseph Anointing

Friend, settle in close. Let's share this table again, heart to heart—like breaking bread beside the fire of His presence. There's a story unfolding that carries your name, a story that whispers destiny through every detour. Joseph's life isn't just ancient history; it's a prophetic mirror reflecting what God is doing right now in those who will endure. His journey declares that your environment does not define your destiny— presence does. From the pit to the prison to the palace, Joseph faced betrayal, injustice, and delay, yet the same refrain echoed through every season: *"The Lord was with Joseph."* (Genesis 39:2, 21)

That is the essence of the Joseph anointing. It is not the absence of hardship but the triumph of presence in the midst of it. It is the power to shine in darkness, to carry peace in chains, to host heaven in hostile places. This anointing builds upon what we've just seen in Chapter 3—the law of beholding. When you fix your eyes on Jesus, you begin to carry His likeness; when you endure through fire, that likeness becomes unshakable. What we behold transforms us, but what we endure refines us. And through it all, Holy Spirit is forming a generation who will not bend under pressure but burn with purpose.

So come—let's walk the road with Joseph. Let's trace the fingerprints of God through betrayal, injustice, and delay, and discover how endurance becomes the forge of glory. Because this story isn't just about him—it's about you. It's about what heaven is doing right now in a generation being prepared for famine and revival alike. This is the hour of the Joseph anointing—when dreamers are being refined into deliverers, and those who've been buried are about to rise above the sun.

The Pit: Resilience in Betrayal

Picture Joseph at seventeen—the dreamer clothed in a coat of many colors (Genesis 37:3). That garment was more than fabric; it was a prophetic banner announcing destiny. Yet favor often provokes envy. His brothers stripped it away, threw him into a pit, and sat down to eat while his cries echoed from the darkness (Genesis 37:23–25).

The cruelty is staggering—family feasting while the favored one weeps in a hole. Betrayal by those who should have loved him most always cuts the deepest.

But hear this truth: the pit was never meant to bury Joseph's destiny; it was meant to reveal it. The pit is the great equalizer. It strips away titles, applause, and outward symbols until only one question remains—Will you trust the God of your dream when the dream looks dead?

The pit reveals whether your faith is built on circumstances or on covenant.

Many have felt this same descent—the sudden plunge from promise into silence, from favor into misunderstanding. The whispers come quickly: You're forgotten. You're finished. Your dream was foolish. Yet heaven's verdict still stands: *"The Lord was with Joseph."* (Genesis 39:2)

That single line rewrites the story. The Lord was with him—
not after the betrayal, but in it. God never steps back from
your pain; He steps into it.

The pit becomes the birthplace of resilience. There, stripped
of every prop, you learn that God's presence is your true
covering. You discover that destiny is not held in a coat of
favor but in the fire of faith.

The pit whispers of endings, but in God's language it means
beginning. It is not the grave of purpose but the gateway to
refinement. Those who descend into it and still lift their eyes
to heaven rise with authority that cannot be shaken.

So, friend, if you find yourself in a pit—betrayed, overlooked,
silenced—take heart. You are not buried; you are being
planted. And planted things do not stay hidden forever.

They break through the soil in due time, stronger, deeper,
radiant with life.

Even here, the Lord is with you.

Pause for a moment and let that settle in your spirit:

The same presence that hovered over Joseph in the pit is
hovering over you now.

Potiphar's House: Integrity in Injustice

Dragged from the pit, sold into slavery, Joseph arrives in Egypt stripped of his family, culture, and identity. To the natural eye, it looks like demotion—a dreamer reduced to a servant. Yet Scripture anchors us again with that same refrain:

"The Lord was with Joseph, and he became a successful man." (Genesis 39:2)

This is the paradox of the Joseph anointing: your surroundings may change, but your source does not.

Favor is not bound to location. Anointing is not limited by circumstance. The presence that walked with Joseph in the pit walked with him into Potiphar's house, turning captivity into stewardship.

Even as a slave, Joseph rose in trustworthiness until Potiphar placed everything under his care. His excellence wasn't ambition—it was worship. His faithfulness in small things revealed a heart that served heaven even when earth forgot him.

That's the hidden strength of this anointing: God's favor rests most visibly on those who serve faithfully in unseen places.

But then came the test. Potiphar's wife cast longing eyes on Joseph and whispered, *"Lie with me."* (Genesis 39:7)

Temptation rarely announces itself as destruction—it disguises itself as relief, comfort, or validation. Day after day, Joseph refused, not because of fear of consequence, but because of covenant:

"How then can I do this great wickedness and sin against God?" (Genesis 39:9)

Notice the center of his reasoning: not Potiphar, not reputation—God.

Integrity always flows from intimacy. The fear of the Lord guarded Joseph when no one was watching.

And though his obedience was pure, the result looked unjust. Falsely accused, Joseph was thrown into prison; his garment once again torn away, his name dragged through the mud. It's one of Scripture's hardest truths—doing right doesn't always lead to immediate reward.

Sometimes, it leads to deeper refining.

But remember this: injustice is never the end of the righteous.

Heaven records what men forget. The world may strip away position, but it cannot touch purity. Potiphar's wife could grab Joseph's cloak, but she could never steal his calling.

Every accusation became an opportunity for endurance. Every false word became fuel for the fire of destiny. What looked like demotion was divine direction—the Lord was still with Joseph.

Perhaps you've faced something similar—maligned for telling truth, misunderstood for obeying God, punished for standing for what is right. Don't let bitterness take root. The God who writes your story wastes nothing.

He is watching how you respond in the shadows. Before He promotes you in public, He tests you in private.

Integrity in injustice is heaven's proving ground.

If you can stand when lies fly and keep your gaze on God when reputation shakes, you are being fitted for greater authority.

The Joseph anointing is not about escaping trials—it's about carrying purity through them, trusting that vindication belongs to the Lord.

So when you're wronged, resist the urge to fight in the flesh.

Stay faithful. Stay pure. Stay present in His presence.

The same Spirit who sustained Joseph in Potiphar's house is preparing to lift you through your own testing.

What you lose for righteousness today will one day become the garment of honor heaven places upon you.

The Prison: Endurance in Delay

Chains clanged shut. The dreamer who once wore a royal coat now wore shackles. The same man who carried favor in Potiphar's house was led away as a prisoner. To human eyes, Joseph's story looked finished—favor forgotten, promise postponed, destiny delayed.

But heaven's record still reads the same:

"The Lord was with Joseph and showed him steadfast love and gave him favor in the sight of the keeper of the prison." (Genesis 39:21)

That sentence defies logic.

God's steadfast love in a cell? Favor in confinement?

Yes—because presence is not a product of freedom.

The Joseph anointing carries the mystery of endurance: God's favor is not absence of trial; it is strength within it.

In the darkness of that prison, Joseph did not lose his vision; he served with it.

He interpreted the dreams of others while waiting for the fulfillment of his own.

123 |

That is endurance—continuing to minister even when your own promise seems delayed.

When the cupbearer and baker came to him troubled, Joseph didn't look inward; he looked upward:

"Do not interpretations belong to God?" (Genesis 40:8)

He acknowledged that gifting is nothing without dependence. Even in chains, he carried divine confidence.

But after interpreting their dreams, the cupbearer was restored—and forgot him.

Days turned to months. Months into years. Silence thickened. The Scripture sums it up in four haunting words:

"Yet the chief cupbearer did not remember Joseph, but forgot him." (Genesis 40:23)

That's where many lose heart—in the stretch between revelation and remembrance.

Delay whispers that God has stepped away, but He hasn't.

He is working in the unseen, weaving timing into transformation.

Delay is not denial; it is divine design.

Psalm 105:19 says, *"Until what he had said came to pass, the word of the Lord tested him."*

The promise itself became the refining fire. The same word that once inspired him now invited him to trust beyond sight. And this is the essence of endurance—to keep believing when the evidence has vanished.

If you find yourself in that place—forgotten, waiting, wondering—hear the Spirit's whisper: You are not forsaken. The silence is not punishment; it's preparation.

Heaven has not stopped writing; God is sharpening your pen through waiting.

In delay, He forges discernment. In hiddenness, He builds humility. In silence, He cultivates authority that can carry glory without pride.

The prison is not a tomb. It is the workshop of destiny. God is shaping in you what cannot be formed in palaces—steadfastness, trust, patience under pressure, and faith that thrives in the dark. Then, at the appointed time, the door swung open.

Pharaoh's call came, and the dreamer was summoned. It looked sudden—but it was years in the making.

Heaven's timing never rushes, never lags; it arrives at the moment when maturity and mission finally meet.

So wait well. Serve faithfully. Worship in your waiting. Because the same presence that was with Joseph in prison is with you in your delay. And when the season shifts, you will see that every moment of confinement was really the corridor of preparation. He who called you is faithful, and in His time, He will open the door no man can shut.

The Palace: Destiny in Promotion

And then, suddenly—it happened.

One summons from Pharaoh changed everything. The same man forgotten in prison woke that morning surrounded by chains and went to bed clothed in royal linen. The shift was breathtaking, but it wasn't random. Heaven had been preparing this moment all along.

Pharaoh had dreamed two dreams no magician could interpret. Fear spread through the palace like smoke, until the cupbearer remembered—the one he'd forgotten in the darkness. "I remember my offenses today," he said (Genesis 41:9).

In one sentence, the silence of years broke open, and destiny stepped forward.

Joseph was brought out quickly. He shaved, changed his clothes, and stood before the throne of the most powerful ruler on earth. Pharaoh said, "I have heard it said of you that when you hear a dream you can interpret it."

And Joseph, no longer the brash seventeen-year-old dreamer, answered with humility that dripped with heaven's authority:

"It is not in me; God will give Pharaoh a favorable answer." (Genesis 41:16) That is the language of those refined by waiting—no striving, no self-promotion, no need to prove.

Joseph's years in the pit and the prison had taught him the secret of greatness: presence over platform, obedience over opportunity.

He didn't interpret Pharaoh's dream to secure his release; he did it to reveal God.

As Joseph spoke, revelation flowed. He declared that Pharaoh's dreams foretold seven years of abundance followed by seven years of famine. But Joseph didn't stop at revelation—he released strategy. He advised Pharaoh to appoint overseers to store grain during the good years, so the nation could survive the famine.

Wisdom poured from him like oil, and Pharaoh recognized what no résumé could prove: *"Can we find a man like this, in whom is the Spirit of God?"* (Genesis 41:38)

In a single decree, the prisoner became prime minister. The forgotten servant became the most trusted voice in the land. But make no mistake—the palace did not make Joseph. It revealed what the pit, the house, and the prison had already formed.

Each season had carved something sacred: The pit taught resilience when betrayal tried to bury him. Potiphar's house forged integrity when temptation tested him. The prison built endurance when delay stretched him. And now the palace unveiled purpose when destiny called him. That is the pattern of divine promotion—it always follows formation.

God lifts you not to decorate you with status but to delegate responsibility.

Every trial is rehearsal for rulership. Every hidden season trains you to carry public authority without losing private humility. Joseph's first act in power was not vengeance but provision. He used his influence to preserve life. The famine that could have destroyed nations became the stage for salvation. This is the Joseph anointing—promotion that feeds nations, not egos.

When God elevates, He expects stewardship. When He entrusts influence, He demands purity. The palace is never the goal; it's the platform for purpose. The dream was not for Joseph's comfort—it was for Egypt's survival and for God's covenant to continue.

You may not stand before Pharaoh, but God is preparing a "palace moment" in your life—an assignment of influence, a space where endurance and faithfulness will meet divine opportunity. And when that day comes, remember Joseph's words: *"It is not in me; God will give the answer."*

The true test of promotion is not how high you rise, but how low you bow once you're there. The palace will prove what the pit prepared. So walk softly. Lead wisely. Remember that every door He opens is an altar of assignment.

Your influence exists to preserve life—to bring light where famine reigns, to release strategy when fear grips, to display His glory before kings.

That is the destiny of those who have endured the refining fire: to stand before the powerful, not as servants of men, but as carriers of the Spirit of God.

The Joseph Anointing for This Hour

Joseph's story isn't a relic—it's a revelation. His journey from pit to palace is not just the record of one man's endurance; it is the prophetic blueprint for a generation being prepared right now.

We are living in a time that mirrors his world—an age of betrayal, injustice, and delay. The same forces that tried to silence Joseph are at work again, yet the same refrain thunders through history: *"The Lord was with Joseph."*

Betrayal has multiplied—families fractured, covenants broken, trust traded for convenience. Injustice has become institutional—truth mocked, righteousness labeled intolerance, holiness dismissed as hate. Delay hangs heavy—prayers unanswered, revival promised but not yet seen.

But into this swirl of confusion, Holy Spirit is releasing a familiar fragrance—the Joseph anointing—the grace to carry God's presence through pain, to stay faithful under pressure, and to turn famine into fruitfulness.

This anointing rests on those who will not bow to bitterness when betrayal comes. On those who will not compromise integrity when injustice strikes. On those who will not quit believing when delay stretches their soul. It is the mantle of those who can steward favor without pride, and endure suffering without despair.

Joseph's life was not preserved for comfort; it was positioned for preservation. He carried grain in a time of famine—heaven's supply for a starving world. That is what the Spirit is forming again in this hour—a Joseph generation, chosen to feed nations, not with wheat, but with revelation, truth, and hope. Look around—can you see the famine? It's not just economic; it's spiritual. A famine of truth, where deception fills the airwaves. A famine of love, where betrayal masquerades as freedom. A famine of hope, where despair has become fashionable and cynicism a badge of honor. But in the midst of it, God is raising modern Josephs—men and women whose hearts have been refined in secret fire, whose endurance has been forged in hidden years, who can stand before Pharaohs of culture and carry solutions born from communion with God.

This is the call of the Joseph anointing: To walk in prophetic wisdom when the world panics. To feed souls when systems fail. To govern with grace when corruption collapses. To shine with integrity when compromise becomes common.

The Joseph anointing is not about survival—it's about stewardship. It's not the escape from famine; it's the assignment to feed it. Those who have endured betrayal are being entrusted with reconciliation. Those who have faced injustice are being equipped with mercy. Those who have walked through delay are being anointed with patience to lead others through waiting.

It's happening now—in classrooms, in boardrooms, in pulpits, in homes. Young dreamers are being tested in pits of obscurity. Hidden intercessors are interpreting the dreams of leaders. Mothers, fathers, pastors, and business owners are carrying supernatural strategy that will preserve life when the world shakes again. They may look ordinary, but the Spirit of God rests upon them. You can feel the stirring even now— the shift in the atmosphere. Heaven is aligning timelines.

The Spirit is whispering: *"What men meant for evil, I am turning for good."* The Joseph generation will not retaliate; they will redeem. They will stand before their accusers and say, *"You meant it for harm, but God meant it for good—to save many alive."*

That's the anthem of this hour.

And it belongs to those who choose presence over position, purity over platform, and purpose over pain. So, if you've been misunderstood, betrayed, or delayed—don't despise it. You're not being punished; you're being positioned. Your story is being woven into something global and glorious.

The famine is here, but so is the grain. And the storehouses of heaven are opening through the lives of those who endured without losing their fire.

This is the hour for Josephs to arise—carriers of wisdom, stewards of presence, and preservers of life. Your pit will become your platform. Your prison will become your proving ground. And your palace will become your pulpit. Because the same Spirit who was with Joseph in every season is the Spirit being poured out on you now.

Betrayal, Injustice, Delay: God's Greater Plan

Every strike of Joseph's life carried pain—but every wound carried purpose. The betrayal, the false accusation, the forgotten years—all of it formed the foundation for a single revelation that silences hell: *"You meant evil against me, but God meant it for good, to bring it about that many people should be kept alive."* (Genesis 50:20)

Those words were not born in comfort; they were forged in captivity. They did not come from theory; they came from tears. Joseph said them standing before the very brothers who stripped him, sold him, and lied about his death. And yet, what came out of his mouth was not revenge, but revelation.

He had seen the pattern of heaven woven through his pain. He had lived long enough to realize that what men intend for destruction, God repurposes for redemption.

This is the mystery of divine sovereignty—the furnace that forms deliverers. Betrayal refines compassion. Injustice purifies motive. Delay matures discernment. And together they weave the character required to carry glory without distortion.

What looked like the enemy's triumph became heaven's training ground. The pit was not a punishment; it was the proving of faith. Potiphar's house was not humiliation; it was hidden promotion. The prison was not abandonment; it was apprenticeship for authority. Every season, though dark, was sacred. Every delay, though painful, was prophetic.

Psalm 105:19 gives the secret: *"Until what he had said came to pass, the word of the Lord tested him."*

That word tested means refined by fire. The very promise Joseph carried was the fire that purified him. He had to learn to trust the God of the dream when the dream looked dead.

Have you ever felt that? The ache of waiting for something God Himself promised you, while everything around you screams that it will never come? That's where Joseph lived— and that's where the Joseph generation is forged. Because before God fulfills His word through you, He fulfills His word in you.

Betrayal is the fire that burns off dependence on approval. Injustice is the chisel that shapes humility. Delay is the anvil that strengthens endurance. Each blow that feels like loss is actually the sound of construction.

This is why you can't curse the season that hurts you. The very place that bruises you is the ground that births you. The hands that tried to bury you are unknowingly sowing you.

And planted things do not stay hidden—they rise.

When Joseph's brothers stood trembling before him, expecting wrath, they received mercy instead.

Forgiveness flowed from the same heart that once cried in the pit. That's when we know the refining has done its work—when vengeance turns into vision, when pain becomes provision, when the victim becomes the vessel.

Hear this, friend: *Every betrayal that cut you was a lesson in trust. Every injustice that pressed you was a test of endurance. Every delay that stretched you was a setup for timing. None of it was wasted.*

You may not see the pattern yet, but heaven's loom is never idle. Threads of pain are being woven into garments of glory. You may be standing in the middle of the story, but God has already seen the end. The word that tested you will soon crown you. The places that broke you will become altars where others are fed. This is the Joseph anointing—to see purpose where others see pain, to find redemption where others find regret, and to feed nations from the very field that once felt barren.

So lift your eyes. Your betrayal will not bury you—it will deepen you. Your injustice will not define you—it will refine you. Your delay will not defeat you—it will prepare you. For what the enemy meant for evil, God has already meant for good. And when you stand on the other side—when the dream breathes again, when restoration unfolds, when the famine turns to feast—you will say, with tears and triumph: "He was with me the whole time."

The Church's Mandate: Shine in the Dark

The Joseph story has never been more urgent than now, because its purpose is not personal comfort—it's global commission. What God forged in Joseph's secret years, He is now awakening in His Church. The famine is here—not of food, but of truth. The darkness deepens, yet the call is clear: shine.

This is our hour, not to retreat into nostalgia or hide behind religious walls, but to rise in radiant authority as sons and daughters who know who they are.

Jesus said, *"You are the light of the world. A city set on a hill cannot be hidden."* That declaration wasn't poetic—it was prophetic. The Church is that city. We are the storehouses of revelation in a world starving for meaning. The Joseph anointing now rests corporately on a people who will carry bread for nations, wisdom for governments, and compassion for a culture starving for hope.

This is not the era of celebrity Christianity—it is the era of consecrated community.

The Spirit is calling forth a people who have no need for platforms because they have learned presence; who do not seek applause because they burn for purity; who have been tested in secret so they can steward public influence without compromise.

The Church's light is not a performance—it's a Presence.

We shine when we host Him. We illuminate when we live from the throne room. We conquer darkness not by argument but by abiding.

In the days ahead, deception will look persuasive, compromise will look compassionate, and darkness will masquerade as enlightenment. But the true Church will discern. She will not be silenced by fear or diluted by comfort. Her purity will pierce through pollution. Her worship will shake foundations. Her unity will disarm principalities.

This is the Joseph generation rising again, now embodied as the global Bride of Christ—refined by betrayal, matured through delay, and awakened by the famine of truth. We were never called to survive the darkness; we were called to define it.

The world will not be transformed by louder outrage but by brighter light. And light does not argue with darkness—it simply shines.

That's our mandate: to shine until cities tremble with conviction, until governments encounter mercy, until prodigals see the Father's face in our love.

The days of entertainment faith are over.

This is the hour of encounter faith—of holiness and hunger, of revival that doesn't fit programs, and of communities that mirror heaven's culture. The Church that will stand in this generation is not the one that adapts to the world, but the one that ascends above it.

Look up, Bride of Christ. You are not small; you are radiant. You were born for this midnight. You are the city on the hill Joseph dreamed of, the storehouse filled with living bread. The famine is real, but so is the fire. And that fire lives in you.

So rise, sons and daughters of light. Tend your lamps. Trim the wick. Let oil flow again. For this is the hour of awakening, and the Spirit of the Lord is saying,

"Arise, shine, for your light has come, and the glory of the Lord rises upon you."

From Storehouse to Nations — A Global Call to Action

The Joseph story doesn't end in Egypt's palace; it begins there. The storehouses were never built for luxury—they were built for legacy. And the grain Joseph gathered in secret wasn't meant to be guarded behind palace gates—it was meant to be given. His stewardship became salvation. His obedience became the bridge between famine and fulfillment.

So it is with the Church in this hour.

We have been storing revelation, worship, and truth in the hidden places of prayer. We have been forged in betrayal, refined through injustice, and tested in delay—all to carry something that can feed nations in their famine. What we've gathered in obscurity, heaven is now commanding us to release.

The famine is no longer distant; it is here. Not a famine of bread, but of truth. Not of water, but of hearing the Word of the Lord. And the nations are knocking—hungry for meaning, desperate for hope, starving for the Presence.

This is the hour the Joseph generation was prepared for. It's time to open the storehouses. It's time to pour out what's been hidden, to release what's been refined, to offer what's been forged in the fire of endurance.

We cannot shrink back into preservation when God is calling us into multiplication. We cannot hide our light when the world is drowning in shadows. We cannot keep our grain when the hungry are at the door.

The time of preparation has given way to the hour of release.

The Spirit is moving again through the Church like wind through a field of grain, whispering: *"Open the storehouses. Feed the nations. Carry My presence into famine."*

And just like Joseph, this begins not with abundance—but with surrender. Not with applause—but with obedience. Not with platforms—but with presence.

This is the Church's hour to step forward—not polished, but pure. Not famous, but faithful. Not self-assured, but Spirit-filled.

The same God who positioned Joseph in Egypt is positioning His sons and daughters now—in classrooms, boardrooms, neighborhoods, and nations—to preserve life when everything around them is starving for truth.

What has been refined in secret is about to be revealed in power. The harvest is ripe. The famine is deep. And the Father is saying once again, *"Open the storehouses. Feed My people. Shine in the dark."*

My Story: Finding God in the Waiting

Waiting has been one of the defining markers of my life—not as punishment, but as a tutor. It has been the sacred classroom where God forged me, tested me, and met me in ways success never could. Like Joseph, I've walked through accusation, injustice, and delay—and each has left its mark upon my soul.

I have tasted dishonesty from those who should have been closest—family, friends, people I trusted. Words twisted, motives misjudged, relationships broken. The sting was sharp, echoing Joseph's cries when his brothers stripped him of his robe and mocked his dreams.

I have endured injustice—moments when standing for truth meant being slandered, misunderstood, or even punished. Like Joseph in Potiphar's house, I carried consequences for things I didn't do. Everything in me wanted to defend myself, but Holy Spirit whispered: *"Your integrity carries weight in heaven, even when it costs you on earth."*

And I have sat in the long ache of delay—years of promises hanging in suspension, prayers that felt unanswered, doors that refused to open. Like Joseph forgotten in prison, I too have wondered, *"Lord, did I hear You right? Have You left me here?"* The silence of those seasons pressed hard against my faith.

But here's the mystery I've learned: those very places—betrayal, injustice, delay—became altars where I met God more deeply than ever before. Waiting turned out to be holy ground. Psalm 27:14 became my lifeline: *"Wait for the Lord; be strong, and let your heart take courage; wait for the Lord."* I began to see waiting not as wasted years, but as sacred preparation.

I remember one night of despair when Holy Spirit whispered to my heart, "Your pit is not punishment—it's preparation. Your delay is not denial—it's design. What feels like a prison is a palace in disguise, for I am with you." That word steadied me. Joseph's journey was no longer just a story in Genesis—it became the map of my own soul.

Over time, the truth of Joseph's words has proven faithful: *"You meant evil against me, but God meant it for good"* (Genesis 50:20). What was intended to wound became a place of compassion. Injustice refined trust. Delay produced endurance that quick success never could.

This truth reshapes how we understand legacy. There are seasons when separation lingers, when reconciliation has not yet arrived, and when love must be carried without access. These spaces ache—but they are not empty. Even here, God is at work. Longing is never wasted in His hands.

What feels like waiting becomes preparation. What feels like silence becomes intercession. Seeds sown in prayer, words entrusted to God, and faithfulness practiced in hidden places all carry prophetic weight. They speak to futures we may not yet see, but which heaven is already tending.

Joseph's story reminds us that legacy is not built only through proximity—it is formed through faithfulness. What we steward in the waiting becomes the ground where restoration will one day bloom.

Waiting also gives birth to things that could never be formed in comfort. Vision is clarified in the fire. Calling is refined in obscurity. What feels like confinement becomes the very place where destiny is written. This is often how God works—with all of us. He forges something in the hidden place that becomes nourishment for others in a future season.

Again and again, this pattern reveals itself. Those who have been betrayed yet choose worship discover an unshakable joy. Those who have been falsely accused yet refuse bitterness find authority forged in truth. Those who endure injustice without surrendering their hearts often emerge carrying discernment, strength, and spiritual authority that cannot be taught—it must be tested.

These are Joseph moments. Painful. Purifying. Purposeful. Moments where heaven is not absent, but actively at work—reordering motives, strengthening roots, and preparing vessels for influence that rests on character, not recognition.

So when I write about the Joseph anointing, I am not writing from theory. I am writing from the understanding that waiting leaves marks—some that ache, and others that sing. From nights where silence teaches you how to listen. From mornings where endurance becomes praise. From discovering that God is present even in the places we once believed were abandoned.

This is why legacy matters so deeply. Waiting teaches us that the truest treasures are not built in palaces, but forged in prisons. They are not measured by applause, but by faithfulness. They are carried forward through prayer, through words entrusted to God, and through lives surrendered to purposes larger than themselves.

Like Joseph, we can say, *"God sent me ahead of you to preserve life"* (Genesis 45:5). That is the call of waiting—not merely to endure for our own sake, but to carry presence and promise for those who will come after us.

The Prophetic Call to Endure

Holy Spirit is whispering across the earth: *"Lift your eyes. Your environment does not define you. I am with you, shaping you to shine. Endure, for I am writing your story for My glory."*

This is your moment—do not let betrayal, injustice, or delay dim your fire. Like Joseph, carry God's presence through the darkness. Endurance is not passive waiting; it is active trust. It is faith that refuses to surrender when sight fails. It is holy defiance in the face of despair—the kind that looks into the storm and still says, *"My God is faithful."*

Endurance is the sound of heaven's resistance echoing through human weakness. It is the strength that sings in silence, the courage that waits when others run. Endurance is the seed of revival, the backbone of reformation, and the proof of divine partnership.

The Joseph generation rising in this hour will not be marked by comfort, but by constancy—those who hold steady in shaking, who carry peace through persecution, who love truth when it costs them everything. They will not bow to bitterness when betrayed, nor compromise in the face of injustice. They will not quit in delay. They will live as walking altars of presence—those who have learned to dwell with God in the pit so they can reign with Him in the palace.

Christ's return is near, and the world trembles beneath the weight of groaning creation. Nations rage. Systems shake. The love of many grows cold. Yet in the midst of darkness, the Lord is raising up a people who will burn through the night— those who carry endurance as their oil and intimacy as their flame.

Jesus Himself spoke of this hour: *"But the one who endures to the end will be saved. And this gospel of the kingdom will be proclaimed throughout the whole world as a testimony to all nations, and then the end will come."* (Matthew 24:13–14)

This is that generation. The gospel will not advance on mere enthusiasm but on endurance—through those who have been tested and proven faithful.

Endurance is the hidden fire that fuels revival. It is the unseen strength behind every story of redemption. It's what carried Noah through ridicule, Moses through wilderness, David through exile, Daniel through Babylon, Esther through fear, and Joseph through prison. And it's what will carry you.

So pause here. Feel the weight of the call.

Endurance is not glamorous, but it is glorious. It is not loud, but it is eternal.

Heaven records every tear that falls in faith, every prayer whispered in silence, every moment you choose hope when despair mocks you. These are the victories unseen by men but celebrated by angels.

Let this declaration rise in your spirit: *"I will not bow to bitterness. I will not surrender to fear. I will endure by His presence, and I will shine through the storm."*

Endurance is worship. It is warfare. It is witness. It is the fragrance of those who refuse to give up until the King returns.

A Vision for the Joseph Generation

I see it—a people emerging from the hidden places of refinement, faces marked by firelight, hearts steady in the storm. They have weathered betrayal without losing compassion, walked through injustice without surrendering integrity, and endured delay without abandoning hope. They are the Joseph generation, a remnant refined in the furnace of affliction yet radiant with the presence of God.

They are not defined by titles or platforms, but by purity and endurance. Their authority is not borrowed from institutions, but born of intimacy. These are the ones who have learned to interpret dreams in the dungeon, to sing in the midnight cell, to forgive from the throne. They have discovered the secret Joseph carried—that the Lord was with him in every season—and that awareness has become their unshakable foundation.

I see them in every nation—young and old, male and female, hidden and visible—carrying grain in their hands and glory in their eyes. Their barns are not filled with wheat, but with wisdom; their storehouses are not physical, but spiritual. They carry revelation for famine, discernment for chaos, and peace for trembling hearts. When others panic, they strategize with heaven. When the world runs dry, they pour from the oil of intimacy.

They are students who burn for revival in dorm rooms and classrooms, lifting hands in prayer while others scroll in despair.

They are business leaders who refuse to bow to corruption, carrying integrity as their banner and righteousness as their currency. They are mothers and fathers who disciple their homes like altars, turning mealtimes into communion and children into arrows of light. They are pastors and prophets who have shed ambition for authority, preaching truth without compromise and mercy without fear.

This Joseph generation will feed the famine of the age.

They will carry hope where there is none, truth where deception reigns, and mercy where judgment has run dry. Like Joseph, they will not hoard what heaven gives—they will distribute it. Their storehouses will become sanctuaries of sustenance, feeding nations with the Word of the Lord.

And when the world trembles under the weight of crisis, they will stand—not with arrogance, but with assurance. They will know that the same God who was faithful in their pit will be faithful in their palace. Their influence will not come from striving but from stillness; their promotion will not come from men but from God.

This generation is not distracted by the noise of Babylon. Their eyes are fixed above the sun, beholding the King. They have endured enough to recognize counterfeits, suffered enough to steward compassion, and waited long enough to carry weight. Their language is worship, their weapon is wisdom, and their legacy is life.

I hear the Spirit saying: *"I am raising up a people who will stand in famine and feed nations. They will carry My counsel into chaos, My peace into pressure, My truth into trembling systems. Their endurance will be the platform upon which I display My glory."*

So rise, sons and daughters of endurance. The Joseph anointing rests upon you—not for survival, but for assignment. You have not been hidden to be forgotten; you have been hidden to be prepared. You are being positioned to preserve life in the hour of shaking.

Let this vision steady your heart: When the world sees famine, you will see fullness. When others see endings, you will see beginnings. When the enemy plots destruction, you will release preservation.

This is the call—to live radiant in resilience, humble in power, and steadfast in faith. To be the remnant that carries glory through the storm until the King returns.

The Joseph generation is rising—and you are part of it.

For Today: A Prophetic Invitation to Endure

Beloved, this is not a distant call—it is your invitation, right here, right now.

Heaven is searching the earth for those who will not bow to despair, who will not trade presence for comfort, who will not abandon faith when the waiting grows long. The Spirit of the Lord is moving across the shaking of nations, whispering to hearts made tender by trial:

"Endure with Me. Stay steady. I am building something in you that will outlast the storm."

Your pit is not punishment; it is preparation. Your prison is not abandonment; it is alignment. Your delay is not denial; it is design.

The Joseph anointing is not about escape—it's about endurance. The fire that forged Joseph's heart is the same fire the Father is using now to forge His Church. Every wound has been a classroom. Every silence has been a sermon. Every hidden season has been heaven's workshop shaping endurance into your bones.

This endurance is not weakness—it is worship. It is how heaven defines strength: the ability to keep standing when everything in you wants to sit down. It is the quiet "yes" whispered through tears. It is the faith that still sings, *"Even if He slays me, yet will I trust Him."*

So, stand in your field today—whether it feels like pit, prison, or palace—and know that God is with you.

When betrayal stings, lift your eyes and declare, *"You meant evil against me, but God meant it for good."* (Genesis 50:20)

When injustice rises, anchor your soul in the truth, *"If God is for us, who can be against us?"* (Romans 8:31)

When delay wears you down, cling to His promise, *"Wait for the Lord; be strong, and let your heart take courage."* (Psalm 27:14)

Every time you trust instead of retaliate, you preach a sermon louder than words. Every time you choose faith over fear, you become a signpost of glory. Every time you endure, you declare to hell itself: *"The Lord was with me—and still is."*

This is your prophetic call to endurance. This is how you become unshakable. Because endurance is not just surviving—it is shining through the storm with unborrowed light.

So let this prayer rise from your spirit as a declaration of covenant with God in the fire:

A Prayer of Endurance

Lord, I fix my eyes on You. Be with me in the pit, in the prison, and in the palace. When betrayal cuts, teach me to forgive. When injustice stings, teach me to trust. When delay stretches, teach me to wait with worship. Forge my spirit in endurance, my heart in purity, and my hands in purpose.

Let Your presence be my portion and Your glory be my goal. Make my life a witness of faith that cannot be shaken. I am Yours, Lord—wholly, fully, and forever.

Amen.

Friend, this is your hour. Heaven is not asking for speed but for stamina, not for noise but for endurance. Say yes to the fire that forms you. Say yes to the presence that keeps you. Say yes to the anointing that sustains you. You were born for this hour—to endure, to overcome, and to shine above the sun.

The King is coming—and He's calling you to carry His glory.

From Endurance to Empowerment: The Wind That Follows the Fire

Every forge has a purpose, and every flame gives way to wind. The fire of endurance was never meant to consume you—it was meant to prepare you to carry something: the breath of God.

You've walked through the pit, you've endured the prison, and you've seen how presence sustains you in delay. But now, beloved, the Spirit is ready to move you.

There comes a moment in every believer's journey when waiting turns into walking—when the refining gives way to releasing. Joseph endured long years of testing, but when the appointed time came, the same Spirit who kept him in chains lifted him into command. His endurance became his authority. His stillness became his strength. His yielded heart became a vessel through which the wisdom of heaven flowed.

That is where we are now. The endurance that the Spirit has formed in you is not meant to leave you standing still—it's meant to make you sensitive to His movement.

Because endurance without intimacy leads to burnout. But endurance with intimacy becomes wind in your sails.

The same Spirit who comforted you in the pit is now calling you into partnership. The same voice that whispered "wait" is now saying "walk."

You've been refined in the fire—now it's time to move in the wind.

In the chapters ahead, we will step into the mystery of what it means to walk with the Spirit—to live led, breathed, and moved by the Wind of Heaven.

Not striving to earn His presence, but yielding to His rhythm.

Not performing for power, but walking in communion.

Not chasing moments, but carrying His movement.

Friend, the days of passive Christianity are over. The Joseph generation will not only endure—they will flow. They will move as the wind moves, speak as the Spirit speaks, and love as the Father loves.

So take a deep breath. Feel it—the same breath that raised Jesus from the dead lives in you. The waiting has done its work. The wind is rising.

Welcome to **Chapter 5 — The Spirit-Led Life: Walking with the Wind.**

Chapter 5 — The Spirit-Led Life — Walking with the Wind

The same fire that purified you in the waiting is now the wind that will move you forward.

Friend, lean in close. Let's sit at this table together—not rushing, not trying to prove anything—but opening our hearts to the One who made us. You've probably felt it—the pull of this world to live from the outside in. Screens, schedules, appetites, emotions… they tug hard, telling you who you are and what you should do. But that's not who you are. That's not how you were designed.

At your core, you are not first a body, scrambling to survive. You are not even first a soul, tossed by thoughts and emotions. You are a spirit being—breathed into existence by God Himself. You have a soul—your mind, your will, your emotions—that was given to serve your spirit. And you live in a body, which was never meant to rule you but to carry you.

This is divine order: spirit, soul, body. Paul prayed it straight in 1 Thessalonians 5:23: *"May your whole spirit and soul and body be kept blameless at the coming of our Lord Jesus Christ."* He didn't reverse the order, like the world has. He set it in heaven's alignment. When your spirit, awakened by Christ, is in the lead, everything else finds its place.

I can't get away from how Acts 17:28 anchors me: *"In Him we live and move and have our being."* That's not a poetic line—it's the reality of Spirit-first life. In Him, you live. In Him, you move.

In Him, you discover who you really are. Outside of Him, life frays. Inside of Him, life flows.

I've had seasons where my soul tried to take the wheel—emotions storming, fears shouting, intellect overanalyzing. I've had days where my body called the shots—driven by hunger, comfort, or fatigue. And every time, it left me restless and dry. But when I let Holy Spirit rise from within me—leading my spirit to lead my soul and body—there came a stillness, a strength, and a fire this world couldn't touch.

That's what this chapter is about—not religion, not striving, but a return to divine order. Not living from the noise outside, but from the Spirit within. This is how Joseph endured the pit, how David rose from the pasture, how Peter walked on water, how Jesus stood strong in the wilderness. It's how you and I will stand in these days when everything around us shakes.

So let's walk this together, friend. Let's listen to Holy Spirit. Let's climb this mountain path—not just to see the view, but to become the view. Because when you live Spirit-first, you shine above the sun.

Divine Order: Holy Spirit's Blueprint

Friend, if you could peel back all the layers of your life—your routines, your reactions, even your relationships—you'd find a pattern underneath. A blueprint. God etched it into you from the beginning: **spirit, soul, and body**, flowing in that order. That's not just a nice diagram; it's the architecture of life itself.

Your spirit is the lamp Yahweh lit when He breathed into Adam's nostrils the breath of life (Genesis 2:7). It's the eternal spark, the part of you that communes with God, the place where Holy Spirit bears witness that you are His child. Your *soul—your mind, will, and emotions*—was created to serve your spirit, interpreting what God is saying and choosing to walk in it. And your body, fearfully and wonderfully made, was designed to carry His presence into the earth, a temple where His glory dwells.

But you've seen it, haven't you? The order is upside down in this world. Bodies chasing lust, appetites, and endless cravings. Souls ruled by anxiety, pride, and endless self-justification. Spirits starved, silenced, or ignored. That's why people are exhausted—burning out, scrolling endlessly, medicating the ache. The world trains us to live outside-in, when God designed us to live inside-out.

When I wrote *Set Your Mind on Things Above the Sun,* this truth burned so hot in me that it spilled onto every page: **What you focus on, you make room for. What you fear, you empower.** If your body is leading, appetites will rule. If your soul is leading, emotions will whip you around like a storm. But if your spirit is leading, awakened and alive in Christ, everything else falls into place. The chaos outside can rage, but inside you'll find peace.

I've tasted both sides. I remember a season where my emotions called the shots—fear gripped me, anger fueled me, and I made choices out of reaction instead of revelation. It wore me down. But I've also known the sweetness of divine order: mornings where I stopped, stilled my soul, opened His

Word, and whispered, *"Holy Spirit, lead."* The difference was night and day. My spirit took the helm, my soul came into peace, and even my body found strength.

Friend, this isn't theory. This is survival in the days we're living. When lawlessness increases and love grows cold (Matthew 24:12), only Spirit-first living will hold. Divine order isn't a rulebook—it's alignment with heaven. It's how Jesus walked. It's how Joseph endured. It's how the remnant will shine when the world goes dim.

So let me ask you: Who's leading in you right now? Is your body setting the pace, your soul calling the shots—or is your spirit, alive in Christ, pulling everything into order? The answer will shape your destiny.

Jesus in the Wilderness: Holy Spirit's Triumph

Do you see it? This blueprint of divine order wasn't left to theory—it was modeled in the life of Jesus Himself. Before He ever preached a sermon, healed the sick, or called disciples, He was tested. *"Full of the Holy Spirit, Jesus was led by the Spirit in the wilderness."* (Luke 4:1) Not dragged by fear. Not driven by hunger. Not chasing ambition. Led.

The wilderness is where order is revealed. It strips away illusions, peels back comfort, and forces the question: What's leading you—spirit, soul, or body?

The enemy came at Jesus in the same order he comes at us:

The body first: "Turn these stones into bread." Feed the craving. Make the body king.

Then the soul: "Throw Yourself down." Appeal to pride, to spectacle, to intellect demanding proof.

Finally, the spirit itself: "Bow down and worship me." Trade your worship for power, sell your birthright for influence.

But Jesus never wavered. He answered not from flesh or fear, but from the Spirit alive with the Word of God: *"It is written…"* Every temptation was met with truth flowing from the spirit first. Hunger didn't lead Him, pride didn't sway Him, ambition didn't define Him. Holy Spirit did.

And when the wilderness season lifted, Jesus came out *"in the power of the Spirit."* (Luke 4:14) That's no throwaway phrase—it's the hinge of history. Spirit-first living turned a barren desert into the launching pad for revival.

I've had my own wilderness moments, friend. Times when I was stripped of comfort, left with nothing but silence and questions. My body craved relief. My soul screamed for answers. But when I let my spirit lead—anchored in His Word, whispering promises into the void—I walked out with something stronger than solutions. I walked out with power.

The wilderness isn't a curse; it's a classroom. It's where divine order is tested, proven, and established. It's where flesh loses its grip and Spirit takes the lead.

So let me ask you—when hunger bites, when pride whispers, when shortcuts beckon, where do your eyes go? To the stone?

To the spectacle? To the throne of the world? Or to the Word of the Living God, where your spirit finds its voice?

Because the wilderness will come. But if your spirit leads, you'll come out not weaker, but stronger. Not empty, but filled with power.

Samson: Flesh-First Failure

If Jesus shows us the power of Spirit-first living, Samson shows us the devastation of flesh-first. His story almost reads like a warning whispered to every generation: *anointing without order will consume itself.*

From the womb, Samson was marked. A Nazirite by covenant, destined to deliver Israel from the Philistines (Judges 13). The Spirit of the Lord stirred him early, giving him supernatural strength—tearing lions apart, carrying city gates, striking down armies. But friend, strength without surrender is tinder without flame control. And Samson's life shows what happens when the body and soul take the driver's seat.

He lusted after forbidden women—Philistine wives, prostitutes, Delilah—letting his body dictate destiny. He let rage steer his choices, retaliating when wronged, burning fields, slaying in anger. He toyed with temptation, revealing his secrets bit by bit, until Delilah pressed him into betrayal. And when his vow was finally broken, the Spirit lifted. Blind, bound, grinding grain in the enemy's house, Samson became a tragic picture of wasted potential.

Yes, in the end, his hair grew back. His prayer rose from the prison of his blindness, and God used him one final time to topple the Philistine temple. But hear me—his greatest victory came at the cost of his life. His anointing was real, but his disorder was fatal.

Friend, do you feel the weight of this? Samson didn't lose because he lacked calling; he lost because he let flesh govern what only Spirit could sustain. He had the oil but no vessel of order to carry it.

And isn't that what we see in our day? Men and women blazing with gifting but undone by lust, anger, or pride. I've known leaders who could preach the heavens open but couldn't conquer their appetites in secret. I've felt the same battle in myself—moments when anger pushed me further than I should've gone, or when pride whispered louder than prayer. Every time the soul or body leads, disorder fractures the call.

Samson's life is a mirror held up to us: will you burn out under the weight of your own cravings, or will you yield to Spirit and carry the fire without being consumed?

If the wilderness tests divine order, then Samson proves what happens when order collapses. It's not just about avoiding sin—it's about who sits at the helm of your being. Spirit, or flesh?

Because the world doesn't need more Samson strength. It needs Spirit-led sons and daughters whose anointing is guarded by surrender, not squandered by appetite.

David & Peter: Spirit-Led Faith and Restoration

Samson shows us the ruin of flesh-led living, but David and Peter remind us that even when failure comes, grace has the final word. Their stories sing the same refrain: *when you fall, turn your eyes back to Him—and Spirit will restore what soul and body tried to steal.*

David, the shepherd-king, stood before Goliath with nothing but a sling and a Spirit-anchored gaze. He didn't size himself against the giant; he sized the giant against his God. His spirit led, and courage flooded him. *"The Lord who delivered me from the paw of the lion and the bear will deliver me from this Philistine"* (1 Samuel 17:37). And with one stone, heaven toppled what earth feared. Spirit-first faith births victories flesh could never win.

But David also stumbled. One night on the palace rooftop, his gaze drifted—like we saw in Chapter 3. Bathsheba's beauty caught his eye, and his soul and body surged ahead of Spirit. Desire ignited adultery, deception birthed betrayal, and eventually blood stained his hands. Friend, notice this: the man after God's own heart fell not because he lacked anointing but because he misplaced his gaze.

Yet David's story doesn't end in ruin. When confronted, he broke—not with excuses, but repentance. *"Create in me a clean heart, O God, and renew a right spirit within me"* (Psalm 51:10). Do you feel it? Spirit reclaimed the helm, repentance reopened the flow, and the same man who fell was restored to sing psalms that still heal nations.

And then Peter—the fiery disciple whose highs and lows mirror our own. He stepped out of a boat on a stormy sea, eyes locked on Jesus, walking on water. Spirit-first faith carried him where flesh had no power. But when his gaze shifted to the waves, fear swelled, and he sank. Only grace lifted him. Later, Peter's soul buckled again—denying Jesus three times, cursing that he even knew Him. Can you imagine the shame? The rooster crowed, and hope must have felt lost.

But grace wasn't done. On the shore after the resurrection, Jesus restored him—not with a lecture, but with love: *"Do you love Me?"* (John 21:17). Three denials, three restorations. And when Pentecost came, Peter—once broken by fear—stood Spirit-filled, preaching with fire, and three thousand were saved in a single day.

Friend, do you see the thread? Samson teaches us the cost of disorder. David and Peter reveal the power of repentance. Failure doesn't disqualify you; it can refine you—if you let Spirit lead again. Flesh may trip you. Soul may sway you. But Spirit can restore you, align you, and set you ablaze once more.

This is the mercy of divine order—it doesn't demand perfection; it invites repentance. It doesn't erase your past; it redeems it. David's psalms rise from failure. Peter's sermons roar from denial. And their lives echo into ours: **When you stumble, turn back quick. Let Spirit reclaim the lead, and destiny will not be lost.**

The Church's Mandate: Restore Divine Order

If David's repentance and Peter's restoration teach us anything, it's this: God doesn't abandon His people when they stumble—He realigns them. And what He does in an individual, He longs to do in His Bride. The Church, like David on the rooftop or Peter by the fire, has had her moments of drifting—eyes on numbers instead of presence, gaze fixed on platforms instead of the cross, soul-led by emotion and body-led by comfort instead of Spirit-led by Yahweh.

But here's the good news: repentance restores destiny, even for the Church. Every time she remembers her first love, every time she lifts her eyes again, Holy Spirit rushes in to realign. Like Peter on Pentecost, the Church can rise from denial into bold declaration. Like David after Bathsheba, the Church can sing again, *"Renew a right spirit within me."*

I've seen it with my own eyes. Congregations that once chased smoke machines and strategies, measuring success by attendance charts, suddenly found themselves on their knees in prayer meetings that stretched for hours. Programs faded, but His presence filled the room. The realignment wasn't cosmetic—it was seismic. People wept, chains broke, and the Spirit's fire returned. It wasn't hype; it was holiness.

Friend, this is the mandate in our hour: not to mirror the world's noise but to embody heaven's order. Spirit first. Soul submitted. Body consecrated. When the Bride lives this way, she shines with a light the world cannot counterfeit.

We're not called to echo the culture's outrage or mimic its trends. We're called to release heaven's rhythm into earth. And the world is starving for it. In a generation drowning in confusion, anxiety, and addiction, the Church must rise—not as another voice in the chaos, but as the steady flame of Spirit-led life.

Picture it: young people fasting in hidden places, not for likes or platforms but for His presence. Parents gathering their children at the table, declaring Scripture, turning their homes into sanctuaries. Leaders laying down ego for humility, refusing to be driven by status, letting Spirit set the agenda. These aren't theories; I've witnessed it. And every time, the atmosphere shifts—hope floods in, healing breaks out, revival begins.

This is the Joseph anointing scaled to the Body: to endure, to carry God's presence into famine, to shine in the dark. This is the David and Peter pattern: when we fall, repent quick; when we're restored, rise bold. And this is the prophetic call for the Church right now: **to realign under Holy Spirit's order and burn with the oil of revival.**

Living Spirit-First in a Broken World

If the Church is being summoned to realign, then you and I must ask: *what does that look like in my day, in my home, in my choices?* Because revival doesn't begin in the sanctuary; it begins in the secret place. It begins when you wake up in the morning and decide who gets the first word—your phone or your Father. It begins when you step into conflict and choose whether your soul reacts in anger, or your spirit responds in peace. It begins in the quiet, hidden decisions no one sees, but heaven records.

Living Spirit-first isn't glamorous—it's steady. It's Spirit before soul, spirit before body, spirit before screens. It's saying, *"I am a spirit being, I have a soul, and I live in a body—so I will not let the lesser lead the greater."* The world flips the order: cravings lead, emotions rule, culture dictates. And we wonder why anxiety rises, why hearts grow cold, why joy feels like a stranger. But when Spirit leads, everything finds its place— your mind clears, your emotions settle, your body submits. The chaos may roar, but your inner man is anchored.

I've lived it. There were mornings when the noise of the world pressed so heavy I could barely breathe. Notifications buzzed, headlines shouted, the weight of unfinished work screamed at me. And yet, when I stilled myself and whispered, *"Holy Spirit, lead me,"* something shifted. My body didn't stop aching, my to-do list didn't disappear, but my spirit rose. Suddenly, peace was louder than pressure. His presence was nearer than the noise.

Try it. Before the scroll, let the Scriptures scroll across your soul. Before the emails, let your spirit send its cry: *"Abba, Father."* When temptation tugs, pause and ask, *"Spirit, what's true here?"* That pause is power. It shifts the weight from reaction to revelation.

Living Spirit-first doesn't mean ignoring your soul or body— it means bringing them into alignment. Your emotions aren't your enemy; they're meant to serve your spirit. Your body isn't a tyrant; it's a temple. Fast a meal and feel the flesh submit.

Sing a song when despair whispers and feel the soul yield. Sit with Scripture and let your spirit breathe until His voice steadies your steps.

This broken world is gasping, friend. Depression climbs, confusion multiplies, people numb themselves with endless noise. But you? You're called to be different. To live from the inside out. To rise above the sun. That's not cliché—that's your lifeline. It's the prophetic rebellion of your day-to-day: choosing presence over pressure, Spirit over soul, eternity over distraction.

And here's the secret: every time you live Spirit-first, you're not just surviving—you're sowing revival. You're carrying oil in your lamp. You're shining in ways you may never see until eternity reveals it. Because when you live Spirit-first in a broken world, you become a signpost that says: *There is another way. There is hope. There is fire that does not go out.*

The Oil of Revival: Spirit-Led Living

These Spirit-first choices may feel small—choosing prayer before a screen, stillness before striving, worship before worry. But in heaven's economy, they are oil. The kind Jesus spoke of when five wise virgins kept their lamps filled, while the foolish ran dry (Matthew 25:1–13). Oil doesn't come cheap—it's pressed, it's costly, it's hidden. You can't borrow it, can't fake it, can't conjure it when the midnight cry sounds. You either have it, or you don't.

Every time you surrender your impulses to Holy Spirit's whisper, a drop of oil fills your lamp. Every time you choose His Word over the world's noise, the flame burns brighter. Every time you realign spirit, soul, and body, you store something eternal. Oil isn't gathered in public moments; it's gathered in secret surrender. And that hidden oil becomes visible fire when darkness thickens.

This is why Spirit-first living is not just personal—it's prophetic. It's preparation for the hour we are in. Revival doesn't come because we sing louder songs or host bigger gatherings. Revival comes because lamps are burning. Because hearts are aligned. Because there is oil enough to sustain fire when the Bridegroom draws near.

I've witnessed this in small rooms—believers who learned to live Spirit-first carrying atmospheres that shift entire communities. I've walked into prayer meetings where the air itself felt thick, alive, because hidden vessels carried oil. No stage, no spotlight—just lamps burning. That's the kind of remnant God is raising.

The Joseph generation we spoke of—those who endure betrayal, injustice, and delay—will need this oil to shine in famine. The Esther generation—those called to stand with courage in the face of death—will need this oil to speak when silence would be safer. The Church in these last days cannot survive on empty lamps. Only those who've been storing oil in the secret place will carry enough fire to pierce the midnight hour.

This is the invitation of Spirit-first living: not survival, but supply. To be a vessel burning with steady fire. To be a forerunner who carries flame into famine. To be a lamp that doesn't go out when the King comes walking into the room.

My Story: Finding Freedom in His Order

I know this oil isn't theory because I've had to buy it myself. There were seasons where my lamp nearly flickered out—not because God had abandoned me, but because I was running on fumes, living more from my emotions and exhaustion than from His Spirit. I was pouring out faster than I was filling up, reacting to demands, to betrayal, to pressure, trying to fix everything in my own strength. The result? Empty. Anointed, yes, but tired. Called, but running on embers.

It was in one of those seasons, when the weight of disappointment sat heavy on me, that I heard Holy Spirit whisper: *"You're out of order. Your soul and body are leading; your spirit is starving. Come back into alignment."* That word cut deep, but it saved me. I began to reorder my days—not around chaos, but around His presence. I would rise in the morning and sit in stillness, not rushing to solve problems, but opening my Bible and praying Psalm 46:10: *"Be still, and know that I am God."* Slowly, my lamp began to fill again. Not instantly, but drop by drop.

I've learned that oil is gathered in obscurity. No one applauded those mornings when I chose prayer over scrolling, or fasting when everything in me craved distraction. But heaven noticed. My soul grew quieter. My body came under discipline. And my spirit began to burn again with clarity and peace. This wasn't self-help; it was surrender. It was the Spirit-first order that God designed.

I've seen the fruit. In moments when storms came—loss, conflict, betrayal—I didn't collapse like before. Something steady carried me, a hidden flame no circumstance could quench. And I realized: that's the difference between an empty lamp and a full one. One burns out when the night grows long. The other shines brighter because it's been fed in secret.

This is why I write with such urgency. Because I know what it is to nearly lose the flame. And I know what it is to find it again—not in striving, but in surrender, in Spirit-led order. My testimony is this: when you let Holy Spirit lead, He doesn't just give you oil—He makes you into a lamp that cannot be hidden.

The Prophetic Call to Realign

This is where the Spirit's voice grows loudest: *"It's time to realign."* I can almost feel the urgency in His tone. Not a suggestion, not a gentle nudge—an alarm in the Spirit. Too many are living out of order, letting their emotions steer the ship, letting their bodies dictate the terms, and then wondering why their spirit feels faint. But the Spirit of the Lord is calling us higher.

Realignment is not complicated—it is costly. It means silencing the noise long enough to hear His whisper again. It means letting your spirit lead, instead of bowing to the tyranny of your soul's moods or your body's cravings. It means saying no to distraction so you can say yes to His presence.

This is not about religion. This is not about rigid schedules. This is about survival in the last days. Jesus Himself said the love of many would grow cold (Matthew 24:12), and I believe the greatest threat to this generation is not persecution but distraction. It's the slow leak of oil in lamps that once burned bright.

But I hear the Spirit saying: *"I am reordering My people. I am calling them back into Spirit-first living. I am cleansing the Bride's lamp, filling her again with oil for the days ahead. Realign now, while it is still day."*

This is not just a call for the individual—it is for the Church. We cannot carry revival on hype or human energy. Programs, platforms, and polished performances will not withstand the shaking. Only lamps filled with oil will shine when the midnight cry comes: *"Behold, the Bridegroom is coming!"*

So here is the summons: lay down the illusion of control. Lay down the false security of busyness. Lay down the lie that emotions or appetites should lead. Stand up in the Spirit and declare: *"Holy Spirit, You lead. My soul submits. My body follows. I am Yours."*

Realignment is the doorway to fire. Order is the pathway to oil. And this is the hour for both.

A Vision for Holy Spirit-Led Remnant

I can see them—clear as day. A people set apart, not because they are perfect, but because they are aligned. Their spirits burn steady like lamps filled with oil, their souls no longer tossed by every emotion, their bodies offered as living sacrifices. They walk through a world trembling with chaos, but they are unshaken, because they are anchored in the order of heaven.

This remnant doesn't look impressive to the world. They are hidden in prayer rooms, fasting in secret, singing in their kitchens, raising hands in school gyms, whispering Scripture into hospital halls. But in the Spirit, they are radiant—torches carried into the midnight hour. They are what Daniel saw when he wrote, *"Those who are wise shall shine like the brightness of the sky above; and those who turn many to righteousness, like the stars forever and ever"* (Daniel 12:3).

I've glimpsed them already—a student who traded late-night scrolling for late-night intercession, and revival broke out in their dorm. A father who set aside the grind to gather his family in worship, and his home became a beacon of peace in the neighborhood. A pastor who refused to build on charisma and instead built on the altar, and his church became a furnace of fire that drew the lost. These are the firstfruits of the remnant.

And I believe with everything in me that you are called to be among them. This is not a spectator vision—it is a summons. The Spirit is marking a generation who will not bow to fear, who will not burn out on distraction, who will not settle for living from the flesh or the soul. They will live Spirit-first, shining above the sun, carrying the oil of intimacy and the fire of revival.

This is the remnant that will stand when kingdoms shake. This is the Bride prepared when the cry comes at midnight. This is the company whose alignment becomes fuel for the billion-soul harvest. And the question is not whether they will rise—the question is whether you will rise with them.

For Today: A Prophetic Invitation to Align

This is the hour. The Spirit isn't asking for tomorrow's yes—He's asking for yours right now. The Josephs endured. The Esthers rose. The remnant is rising. And you are being summoned to live Spirit-first—your spirit aligned with heaven, your soul anchored in truth, your body surrendered as a living sacrifice.

Don't wait for perfect circumstances. Don't wait until you feel ready. The invitation is already on the table: realign, receive the oil, burn with His fire. Step into the rhythm of divine order, and you will discover the freedom, clarity, and strength you've been longing for.

Here's how you can respond today:

- Begin Spirit-first. Whisper His name before you check your phone. Open His Word before you open the world.

- Guard your soul. Take thoughts captive. Refuse to partner with fear or shame. Let His truth be your compass.

- Submit your body. Fast, worship, and rest as acts of love, not duty. Offer every breath as worship.

- Carry His presence. Wherever you go—school, work, family, city—be the lamp that refuses to go out.

And now, let's pray—simple, raw, surrendering:

Prayer

Holy Spirit, I say yes. Lead me into divine order. Awaken my spirit to burn with Your fire, align my soul with Your truth, and sanctify my body as Your temple. Strip away distraction, break the grip of the world, and pour fresh oil into my lamp. Let my life shine with Your glory in this generation. Prepare me for the harvest, for the midnight cry, for the coming King. I am Yours.

This is your moment. Say yes today. Take your place among the remnant. Live Spirit-first, burn above the sun, and carry His fire until the whole earth is filled with His glory.

The Josephs endured. The Esthers are arising. And between them, the Spirit-led remnant will carry oil for the midnight hour—lamps burning, hearts aligned, eyes fixed above the sun.

The King is coming, and He's calling you to walk with the Wind.

Chapter 6 — The Esther Anointing: Courage in the Face of Darkness

The same wind that carried Joseph from prison to palace now breathes through the story of Esther.

Friend, pull your chair in close. Let's sit across this table, heart to heart, and step into a story burning with prophetic fire—Esther's story, a clarion call to rise in this trembling hour. The world is shaking—nations raging, truth under siege, hearts growing cold. Yet Holy Spirit is stirring a flame within you: a summons to stand, speak, and act for such a time as this.

Esther wasn't merely a queen; she was a woman who said yes to God when everything was on the line. Her courage saved a nation—and her story now calls forth a generation.

The Hidden Place — Shaped in the Shadows

Esther's story begins in the shadows, not the spotlight. She was an orphan—her parents gone too soon—raised by her cousin Mordecai in the vast Persian Empire. No palace. No platform. No crown. Just a Jewish girl in exile, learning faithfulness in obscurity.

This is the first thread of the Esther anointing: destiny is often forged where no one is watching. The Spirit of God doesn't need a throne room to shape a queen; He uses the quiet corners, the silent years, the overlooked seasons.

Scripture tells us Esther was *"lovely in form and features"* (Esther 2:7), but it wasn't outward beauty that marked her—it was the unseen hand of God weaving favor into her story long before a crown ever touched her head. Heaven's fingerprints already rested on a life the world had dismissed as ordinary.

Have you felt hidden—unnoticed, unheard, unseen? The hidden place isn't punishment; it's preparation. It's where the unseen yes becomes unshakable strength.

And we are watching that same pattern unfold again in our day.

Back in 2011, prophetic voice *Kim Clement* declared, *"As restoration begins, there shall be a woman who rises—strong in faith, virtuous, beautiful in eyes. I have crowned her, says the Lord, as I crowned Esther."*

At the time, those words sounded mysterious, waiting for their hour. But years later, as nations tremble and voices rise, we can see their reflection.

When tragedy struck in 2025, Erika Kirk emerged from hidden faithfulness into visible purpose—turning personal loss into a national trumpet. She had spent years beside her husband, nurturing family, stewarding covenant, never seeking spotlight. Yet when darkness tried to silence her, courage answered instead. Like Esther stepping from obscurity into history, her hidden obedience had already prepared her heart for this hour.

Her story is not isolated; it is prophetic pattern. Heaven always crowns obedience before man ever notices it.

Could it be that the same hidden shaping is happening in you? The prayers whispered in secret, the faith kept in silence, the tears no one saw—perhaps they are oil being stored for the day of your revealing.

The hidden place is not your burial ground; it's your training ground. When your name is called, courage will already be in you, forged in the fire of faithfulness.

The Palace — Positioned for Purpose

From obscurity to royalty—this is where the Esther story turns. One day she was an exile; the next, she was queen in Persia's courts. What looked sudden was years in the making. Heaven always prepares in secret before it reveals in public.

Esther didn't win her crown through ambition. She listened, yielded, and followed instruction. She carried humility into a place obsessed with appearances, and Scripture says she *"won the favor of everyone who saw her."* (Esther 2:15) Her beauty caught eyes, but her surrender caught heaven.

The palace isn't a prize for ambition; it's a post for assignment. It tests identity, measures motive, and asks one question: Will you use influence for comfort or calling?

Have you recognized your own "palace"—your workplace, your school, your family—as an altar of assignment? You've been positioned, not pampered. Mordecai's words echo through the centuries: *"Who knows but that you have come to your royal position for such a time as this?"* (Esther 4:14)

The Risk — Courage Over Fear

The palace was never meant to be a hiding place—it was meant to be a launch pad. When Haman's decree threatened annihilation, Mordecai's message pierced Esther's comfort: You cannot stay silent now.

She could have withdrawn behind luxury. But the Esther anointing will not let God's people remain silent in the face of darkness.

Her reply changed history: *"Go, gather all the Jews… fast for me… I will go to the king, even though it is against the law. And if I perish, I perish."* (Esther 4:16)

Where is God asking you to risk comfort for obedience? Where is silence tempting you more than surrender? Faith doesn't remove fear—it dethrones it. *"If I perish, I perish"* is not surrender to death; it's surrender to destiny.

The Breakthrough — Deliverance Through Your Yes

When the fasting ended, Esther dressed not for beauty but for battle. She walked toward the throne carrying a nation in her heart. The king's scepter extended—death bowed to obedience.

Breakthrough always follows surrender. Your yes carries more power than strategy, more influence than status.

What if one obedient act could shift the spiritual climate of your family, your church, your city? What if revival is waiting on ordinary people saying extraordinary yeses?

A student who risks ridicule to share faith at school—heaven moves. A parent who begins praying aloud over their children—peace invades. A widow who turns grief into worship—darkness breaks.

These are not rare miracles; they are previews of what happens whenever obedience meets opportunity.

Breakthrough is born when everyday people choose a supernatural yes.

Prayer and Fasting — The Fire of the Call

Esther didn't enter the throne room with clever arguments; she entered clothed in prayer and fasting. Before she touched Persia's throne, she touched heaven's.

For three days she and her people humbled themselves—no food, no drink, no distraction—just desperate dependence on God. That's where courage was forged.

Could it be that courage still waits in that same place today?

When you quiet the noise and make room for His whisper, fear loses its footing. When you fast, you silence the body so your spirit can speak. Fasting terrifies the enemy because it transfers authority. Appetite bows to alignment, and the soul yields to Spirit.

So what might happen if you stepped back from the scroll of your screen, from constant noise and craving, to seek His face? What if hunger became your worship? That's where Esther's fire rekindles—in you.

The Rising Sound — Esther's Fast, Erika's Cry

Fasting births a sound. Esther's obedience thundered across an empire; her life became worship.

That same sound is rising again in our day. It's not polished choirs or performance—it's the raw cry of those whose hunger has become harmony.

And we can hear that cry echo through Erika Kirk's voice. Standing in the ashes of loss, she declared before the world, *"The evildoers responsible have no idea what they have done. You have no idea the fire you have ignited within this wife. The cries of this widow will echo around the world like a battle cry."*

That's not rhetoric—it's *revelation*. It's the roar of an Esther anointing, the same Spirit that turned fasting into fire in the days of Persia. Her words were not crafted for applause; they were born from hidden altars of prayer.

And that cry is multiplying. Across nations, unseen worshipers are lifting the same sound—students in dorm rooms, families around kitchen tables, intercessors in midnight watches. The sound of surrender is filling the earth again.

Can you hear it? Will your life join it? Worship is warfare, and when obedience sings, hell trembles.

The Prophetic Call to Rise

The sound has gone out—but it's more than music; it's a summons.

The same Spirit who stirred Esther now calls His people: Rise. Step forward. Speak truth. Carry My presence into impossible places.

You are not where you are by accident. You were positioned for purpose, refined for risk, anointed for this hour.

Your voice matters. Your courage is needed.

Across the earth, the Esther anointing is awakening again—men and women refusing to bow to fear, choosing holiness over compromise, presence over popularity.

Can you feel it in your bones? The trumpet of heaven still asks, Who knows whether you have come to the kingdom for such a time as this?

A Vision for the Esther Generation

Look closely and you can almost see them—a generation rising with Esther's fire in their bones. They are not swayed by applause or silenced by intimidation. Their eyes burn with love; their mouths carry truth; their hearts beat with courage.

Have you met them? A student fasting three days for her campus, standing unshaken when mocked. A father praying nightly until peace fills his home. A widow declaring that what the enemy meant for death will roar louder in life.

These are not elite heroes; they are first fruits of a movement. This anointing is not reserved for a few—it's an invitation for all.

Teachers in classrooms, leaders in boardrooms, teenagers in prayer rooms—each carrying light into darkness.

Ordinary in the world's eyes, royal in heaven's.

And maybe you are among them. Perhaps your hidden season has been training for this hour.

The Spirit is whispering: You were born for this. Your voice is needed. Your yes is heaven's strategy.

For Today — The Rising Sound and a Prophetic Invitation

There's a sound in the earth right now. It's not perfection—it's passion. The cry of sons and daughters choosing courage over comfort, worship over worry, obedience over fear.

Will your life carry that sound?

Will your voice join the chorus that says, "If I perish, I perish—but I will not be silent"?

This sound isn't noise—it's alignment. It dethrones fear, silences lies, and opens doors for revival.

Here's the invitation, straight from Holy Spirit's heart to yours:

- Trade silence for song—lift His name above the noise.
- Trade complaint for chorus—let gratitude become your weapon.
- Trade fear for faith—declare His promises until peace returns.
- Trade comfort for courage—risk obedience, even when it costs you.

Prayer

Jesus, I say yes for such a time as this.

Tune my spirit to Your sound.

Let my voice echo heaven's truth in a world of lies. Where fear has bound me, set me free.

Where silence has muted me, awaken my song.

I lay my life on Your altar—use it to shake nations.

For Your glory, for Your harvest, for Your name.

Amen.

This is your Esther moment.

Heaven leans in. The scepter is extended.

Your yes is the spark that can light fires in families, cities, and nations.

Never underestimate the weight of obedience. The rising sound is here—now it must rise in you.

The trumpet has sounded. The vision is clear. The wind is rising.

Will you rise—and will you rest?

The Esther anointing calls you not only to stand before kings but to kneel before the Father.

The courage that changes nations is always born in the arms of love.

Chapter 7 — Resting in the Father's Love: The Still Point of All Things

The wind that carried Esther into courage now settles into a holy calm. After the roar of battle and the trembling yes, there comes a whisper—the invitation to rest. Every warrior must learn this rhythm. Every revival must return to relationship. The same Spirit who sends you into fire now draws you back into stillness, reminding you that intimacy is not the reward of obedience; it's the reason for it. You cannot sustain what you do for God without first remembering who you are to Him. This is where the noise fades, the striving ceases, and love becomes the air you breathe. For before you were ever called to stand before kings, you were called to sit at the Father's table.

Rest is not inactivity—it's alignment. It's not the absence of movement; it's the presence of trust. When your soul finally exhales and your striving quiets, something holy begins to happen. The heart of the Father becomes the atmosphere around you. His love doesn't demand performance; it restores identity. His voice doesn't drive; it draws. Rest is where the orphan heart is silenced, and the son or daughter within you awakens again. You realize that your worth was never in what you could do for Him, but in what He has already spoken over you: *"You are Mine."*

This is where every revival must return—to the Father's embrace. The same Spirit who thunders through prophets and empowers the Church also whispers in the stillness, "Come home." Fire without rest burns out; calling without communion collapses. Esther's courage may have saved a nation, but it was intimacy that sustained her spirit. The Father is inviting His people back to that place—the still point beneath the storm—where love becomes the source, not the reward. You can feel it even now: the shift from doing to being, from warring to abiding, from noise to knowing.

This is the secret Esther carried into the throne room. Her three-day fast wasn't about summoning human bravery—it was about leaning into the God who loved her people enough to write their names on His hand. Her *"If I perish, I perish" was* not reckless bravado; it was trust—trust that her life was already secure in the One who holds every heart, even the heart of a king, in His hand (Proverbs 21:1).

And this is where your story turns too. The same Spirit who calls you to rise is the Spirit who whispers, *"Be still, and know that I am God."* (Psalm 46:10) He doesn't just send you into battle; He draws you into His embrace. The fire of Esther's courage must be stoked by the warmth of the Father's love, or else it burns out. To live above the sun—to walk through famine, betrayal, or decree—you must know, not in theory but in the marrow of your soul, that you are loved. Held. Chosen. Safe.

There have been moments when the call of God felt too heavy and the battle too fierce. Yet every time, His love has been the resting place that steadied my feet—not my performance, not my resolve, but His voice, saying, *"You are My son. You are My beloved. You are Mine."*

Before we go further into the Father's embrace, pause here. Take a breath. Let His love wash over you like a river. You don't have to earn it. You don't have to prove it. You only have to receive it. Because what the Father longs to give you is not another assignment—it is Himself.

The Father's Heart: A Love That Runs

Let's linger at one of the most breathtaking windows into God's heart—the parable of the prodigal son (Luke 15:11–32). Don't rush past it. Slow down. Let the dust of that ancient road rise in your imagination. Feel the tension of the scene unfold.

A restless son, weary of home, demands his share of the inheritance before his father has even passed. It's a shocking insult in the culture of the day—essentially wishing his father dead. Yet the father, without argument or resistance, gives it. The son runs headlong into a far country, spending wildly on pleasures that glitter but cannot satisfy. His money dries up. A famine strikes. Soon he's starving in a pigpen—unclean, humiliated, stripped of every illusion.

Here, in the stench of failure, the enemy whispers his oldest lie: "You've gone too far. You're ruined. The Father won't take you back." So the prodigal begins rehearsing his confession—a speech soaked in shame: *"I am no longer worthy to be called your son; make me like one of your hired servants."* (Luke 15:19) He's ready to crawl home as a slave, convinced sonship is lost.

But the story turns on one breathtaking detail.

"While he was still a long way off, his father saw him and felt compassion, and ran and embraced him and kissed him." (Luke 15:20)

Did you catch it? The father ran. In that culture, patriarchs didn't run. To do so meant hiking up their robes, exposing their legs—a public humiliation no dignified man would endure. But this father doesn't care about dignity. His son is coming home, and love outruns propriety. He sprints down the road, throws his arms around the boy, silences the speech of shame, and begins restoration.

"Bring the best robe." Not any robe—the best one. A covering of righteousness over filthy rags.

"Put a ring on his hand." Not jewelry, but authority restored—signet-ring power to act again in the family's name.

"Sandals on his feet." Slaves went barefoot. Sons wore shoes. Identity restored in a single gesture.

"And kill the fattened calf." The feast wasn't just a meal—it was a public declaration: *"This is my son. He was dead and is alive again. He was lost, but now he is found."*

The robe, the ring, the sandals, the feast—every detail is prophetic. They reveal a Father who doesn't merely tolerate your return but celebrates it. He doesn't wait with crossed arms and a list of failures. He runs. He embraces. He restores. His love moves faster than your repentance. His compassion outruns your shame.

And here's the deeper revelation: this story isn't only about a wayward son coming home—it's about the Father revealing who He truly is. Jesus told this parable to dismantle the lie that

God is a distant accountant of sins. No—He is a Father whose heart burns to run to His children.

Maybe you've rehearsed the same speech of shame: "I should have done more. I've failed too many times. Maybe I'll just stay on the edges of His house." But the Father interrupts every speech like that. He wraps His arms around you before you can finish a sentence. He whispers: *"You are Mine. You've always been Mine. You never stopped being My child."*

This is where endurance gets replenished. Joseph endured pits and prisons because he knew the Lord was with him. Esther faced kings because she knew she was loved by a greater one. And you—you can face betrayal, injustice, delay, even death itself, because the Father's arms are your home. His embrace is your rest.

Rest isn't passivity; rest is confidence in the Father's love. Rest is the robe over your shame, the ring on your hand, the sandals on your feet. Rest is the feast that declares, "You belong."

So hear it again—not as a parable for someone else, but as a word straight to your heart: the Father is running. He's already on the road. He's already seen you "a long way off." He's not waiting for perfection; He's waiting for proximity. And when He reaches you, He won't lecture you—He'll embrace you.

This is the Father's heart. This is the love that runs.

Rest vs. Striving: The Orphan's Lie

If the Father's love is a feast, then striving is famine. One overflows with abundance; the other starves the soul. One says, *"You already belong."* The other whispers, *"Prove yourself, and maybe you'll belong."*

This lie of striving is the soundtrack of Babylon. From Genesis to Revelation, Babylon represents humanity's attempt to build significance apart from God—towers reaching for heaven, economies built on oppression, systems forged in fear. Babylon keeps repeating the same lure: *"Work harder. Climb higher. Earn more. Then you'll matter."* And because we have believed it, many of us live not as sons and daughters but as orphans.

The orphan spirit measures worth by output—by hours, numbers, applause, and performance. It's slavery dressed in ambition. But Heaven's economy runs on love, not labor. Sons don't hustle to prove themselves; they rest in the Father's delight and work from identity, not for it.

I once wrote in *Set Your Mind on Things Above the Sun*: *"What you focus on, you make room for; what you fear, you empower."* Striving keeps your eyes locked on scarcity—*If I don't perform, I'll be forgotten.* Rest shifts your gaze to abundance—*The Father rejoices over me with singing. I already belong.* When you choose rest, you unplug from Babylon's machinery and tune your heart to Heaven's song.

Think about it. Striving is what drove the prodigal away in the first place. He wanted to prove himself, to build his own kingdom with an inheritance he hadn't earned. The pigpen was simply the harvest of striving. And even on the way home, shame still pushed him to strive again: *"Make me like one of your hired servants."* But the Father interrupted him: *"No. You're not a servant—you're my son."*

Striving is the orphan's lie. Rest is the child's inheritance.

And make no mistake—rest is not weakness. Rest is warfare. To rest in the Father's love in a culture that worships hustle is to declare, *"I am not of this world. I live above the sun."* Rest is the roar of sons and daughters who know they already belong.

Many of us have carried the weight of striving for years. We chase affirmation, chase success, chase the next open door, hoping the applause will quiet the ache. But applause fades, and emptiness always follows. It's only when the Father whispers, *"You are Mine, and I am pleased with you,"* that the noise stops. His love quiets the striving; His song silences the fear.

Our world today is Babylon on steroids. Social media counts worth in likes and followers. Hustle culture baptizes exhaustion as virtue. Even the Church can slip into it— measuring success by attendance, budgets, and performance. But the Kingdom cuts through it all. Sons don't compete for approval—they live from acceptance. Daughters don't hustle for belonging—they dwell in love.

Zephaniah 3:17 gives the antidote: *"The Lord your God is in your midst, a mighty one who will save; He will rejoice over you with gladness; He will quiet you by His love; He will exult over you with loud singing."*

Imagine it—the Creator of galaxies singing over you. That's the rest Babylon can't offer and the identity the orphan spirit can't counterfeit.

Rest isn't laziness; it's alignment. Rest refuses to bow to Pharaoh's whip or Babylon's scoreboard. Rest says, *"My worth is not in my work. My identity is not in my output. My inheritance is in my Father."*

And here's the prophetic charge: the billion-soul harvest will not be carried by orphans hustling for approval but by sons and daughters resting in the Father's embrace. Only rest produces endurance like Joseph. Only rest fuels courage like Esther. Rest is the oil that keeps lamps burning when the night grows darkest.

This is the invitation of the Father's heart: lay down striving. Silence the orphan's lie. Rest in His delight. Because in these days, rest is rebellion—and rebellion births revival.

The Prodigal Reframed: Identity Restored

Let's walk slowly into the story again. The afternoon sun hangs low, painting the road in dust and gold. A broken son drags himself forward—barefoot, hollow-eyed, clothed in rags that still smell of pigs. Each step carries the weight of failure; each breath rehearses the same desperate speech: *"I am no longer worthy to be called your son. Make me like one of your hired servants."*

That is the orphan's lie in its purest form: You've gone too far. You've ruined too much. You'll never be a child again. Maybe you can survive as a servant.

But the Father—oh, the Father!—is watching the horizon. He's not pacing the porch with arms folded in disappointment or holding a list of conditions. He's scanning the road, heart pounding, eyes fixed on the silhouette of His child. And when He sees that familiar frame, still far off, He does the unthinkable. He runs. He runs through the dust, through the shame, through the stares of those who would judge Him for such undignified love. Love doesn't wait for protocol—it moves first. Mercy outruns sin. Grace crosses the distance. The Father sprints toward the smell of rebellion, collides with the wreckage of His son, and embraces him before a single apology can be finished.

And then the restoration begins.

"Bring quickly the best robe, and put it on him. Put a ring on his hand, and shoes on his feet. Kill the fattened calf. For this son of mine was dead and is alive again; he was lost and is found." (Luke 15:22–24)

The robe wasn't just fabric—it was identity restored. The ring wasn't jewelry—it was authority reinstated. The sandals weren't accessories—they were dignity reclaimed. And the feast wasn't just food —it was belovedness celebrated.

This is the gospel. This is the Father's love. You don't earn it. You don't strive for it. You simply collapse into it, and it restores everything Babylon tried to steal.

And this story is still unfolding in hearts today.

Have you ever recognized the moment when shame loosens its grip—when someone suddenly realizes, *I am still loved*? You can almost feel it when it happens. The striving softens.

The shoulders drop. The eyes lift. Identity begins to speak louder than accusation.

Perhaps you've seen it when someone encounters the truth of adoption—when the words of Scripture awaken something deeper than doctrine: *"You have received the Spirit of adoption as sons, by whom we cry, 'Abba! Father!'"* (Romans 8:15). In that moment, comparison loses its voice. Fear gives way to belonging. It's as if a robe is placed over weary shoulders and a ring is restored to a hand that forgot it was ever chosen.

Or maybe you've recognized it in someone burdened by regret and failure—expecting rejection, bracing for judgment—only to discover welcome instead. A quiet prayer. A gentle reminder of sonship. And suddenly, something shifts. Shame cracks. Hope stirs. It's the Father fitting sandals to tired feet again, teaching His child how to walk upright instead of crawling beneath condemnation.

These moments are not rare exceptions. They are invitations. They are echoes of a story still unfolding in every generation. Because the prodigal's journey is not ultimately about disgrace—it is about discovery. It is about realizing the Father never stopped watching the road.

This is what rest looks like.
Not denial of pain.
Not passivity.
Not escape.

It is identity restored.

Sons and daughters rising into who they have always been—clothed in righteousness not their own, carrying authority they did not earn, learning to live as heirs instead of orphans.

And here is the prophetic truth: the prodigal's story is not only about coming home—it is about becoming whole. It is about hearing the Father's voice declare, *"My child was lost and is found. My child was dead and is alive again."* That is the sound of identity restored—the rest Babylon cannot counterfeit, the oil that keeps your lamp burning, the quiet fire that sustains revival.

The Older Brother: The Danger of Performance

Don't overlook the older brother. He never left home. He never squandered his inheritance. He did everything "right." He worked the fields, followed the rules, stayed close to the house—and yet, when the prodigal returned and the sound of celebration filled the air, something in him broke. Instead of joy, resentment. Instead of gratitude, bitterness.

Listen to his words: *"Look, these many years I have served you, and I never disobeyed your command, yet you never gave me a young goat, that I might celebrate with my friends."* (Luke 15:29)

Do you hear it?

The language of a servant, not a son. I've served. I've obeyed. I've earned. And beneath it all—the unspoken accusation: You owe me.

His heart was just as distant as his brother's, but for a different reason. The prodigal was enslaved by shame; the older brother was enslaved by striving. Both were outside the Father's embrace—one in rebellion, the other in resentment.

This is the quiet danger of performance. You can live in the house of God, serve in His fields, lead His people, preach His Word—and still miss His heart. You can be busy for Him and still not be close to Him.

If we're honest, this mindset seeps into much of today's Church. We measure success by numbers—attendance, budgets, followers, programs—and call it faithfulness. We equate God's approval with visible fruit, not realizing that the Father's delight has never been tied to our production. We find ourselves exhausted, comparing our progress to others, secretly wondering, "What about me, Lord? Haven't I earned it?"

That's the older brother's cry echoing through a modern age of metrics. And it's killing intimacy.

I've seen it in leaders who can't rest, afraid that slowing down means falling behind. I've seen it in worship teams that chase excellence but lose wonder. I've seen it in weary believers who measure holiness by hustle, never realizing that holiness is wholeness—being at home in the Father's love.

The Father's response to the older son is one of the most healing lines in Scripture: *"Son, you are always with Me, and all that is Mine is yours."* (Luke 15:31)

In other words: You don't have to earn what's already yours. You don't have to strive for a place you already have. You're not My servant—you're My son.

It's a whisper cutting through the noise of religion and production: You've been home all along, but you forgot to rest.

This is the moment of awakening the Spirit is bringing to His Church. The Father isn't angry with the older brothers—He's inviting them in. He's calling pastors, parents, leaders, and intercessors out of exhaustion and into enjoyment. Out of pressure and into presence. Out of performance and into communion.

The Father's feast isn't earned—it's entered. And His table is still set.

Babylon demands production; the Kingdom invites presence.

Rest is not passivity—it's alignment. It's the posture that lets you hear the music again. It's stepping out of competition and back into communion. It's realizing that the feast isn't about who deserves it, but about who's willing to come in.

And here's the gentle warning: if we don't confront the older brother within us, we will stay outside the very celebration we were born to join. The Father's arms are open—not to servants who perform, but to sons and daughters who return.

So come in. Let go of the ledger. The music is already playing. The Father is waiting to dance with His children again.

The War for Rest in These Days

Rest is not just relief—it is resistance. It is rebellion against the systems of this age. To rest in the Father's love is to declare war on Babylon, that ancient spirit of striving and performance still seeking to enslave the nations.

Look around. The whole world is addicted to hurry. We measure worth by production, by progress, by performance—grades, numbers, growth charts, and likes. Babylon's lie has woven itself into every rhythm of modern life: You are only as valuable as what you produce.

Students scroll through the night, comparing their reflection to the world's illusion of perfection. Parents labor under endless pressure, believing one more shift, one more zero in the bank, might finally buy them peace. Leaders—both in business and in ministry—burn themselves out, mistaking visibility for vitality and hustle for holiness.

This is more than exhaustion. It is spiritual warfare. Babylon's system runs on fear—you are not enough, and you must prove that you are. The enemy whispers it through algorithms and advertisements, into pulpits and prayer meetings. He knows a restless Church is a powerless Church. Because a people enslaved to performance cannot carry the authority of beloved sons and daughters.

But here is the truth the Spirit is shouting: rest is warfare.

Every time you stop striving and choose to sit in the Father's embrace, you are breaking Babylon's spell. You are declaring: I am not defined by metrics. I am not enslaved to output. I already belong. I already matter. I am already loved.

This was Jesus' invitation when He said, *"Come to Me, all who labor and are heavy laden, and I will give you rest."* (Matthew 11:28)

Those words were not gentle sentiment—they were spiritual defiance. He spoke them to a world ruled by empire and religion, where labor was endless and worth was measured in works. His rest was—and still is—a revolution.

From the very beginning, rest has been God's protest against Pharaoh's whip. When Israel left Egypt, Yahweh's first command was not, "Work harder," but, "Remember the Sabbath." Why? Because Sabbath was resistance. It declared to every taskmaster: We no longer serve you. Our worth is not in bricks and quotas. We are God's people, and He is our source.

That is still the meaning of rest today. Every time you turn off the noise, set down your phone, and lean into His presence, you are confronting the principalities of the age. You are saying, I refuse to live like an orphan when I have a Father who sings over me.

The war for rest is intensifying. Anxiety and depression rates are soaring. Burnout is becoming normal. Identity is unraveling. These are not just psychological crises—they are prophetic signs of a generation under siege. A restless world will consume itself, but a resting Church will carry revival.

And these glimpses are not difficult to recognize. They appear whenever someone chooses presence over pressure.

A young professional, weary of hustle culture, begins to turn a lunch hour into prayer instead of productivity—and peace becomes more compelling than ambition, quietly drawing hearts toward Jesus.

A mother, crushed by expectation, starts whispering Zephaniah 3:17 over her children each night—*"He will quiet you by His love"*—and a new stillness settles into the home. Not forced. Not manufactured. Simply carried by His presence.

A pastor lays down the pressure to perform and returns to adoration—and something shifts. Sermons grow quieter. Hearts grow lighter. And revival begins not through volume or spectacle, but because peace has returned to the pulpit.

This is why The Father's love is not optional—it's strategic. It's survival. It's the way God is waging war on the lie of the age.

Rest is rebellion against striving. Rest is resistance to Babylon. Rest is the roar of sons and daughters declaring, "I already belong."

And that roar is growing.

In Esther's day, fasting was the pause that broke Persia's decree.

In Joseph's Day, delay was the soil that produced deliverance.

And in our day, rest will be the catalyst for harvest.

The Father is raising up a people who will fight differently. Not with frenzy, but with peace. Not with burnout, but with oil. Not with noise, but with stillness that shakes the earth.

So ask yourself—where have you surrendered your rest? Where have you let Babylon set your pace? Because this is the battlefield, and your rest is your weapon.

Lay down your burden. Step out of the noise. The war is already won—now fight it from the place of His peace.

The Father's Love: The Oil of Revival

The war for rest does not end with peace—it ends with power. The Father's love is not merely comfort; it is oil. And without oil, the Bride cannot burn.

Jesus told a story in Matthew 25 about ten virgins waiting for the Bridegroom. All of them had lamps. All of them were invited. But only five carried oil. The others, distracted and unprepared, discovered too late that passion without intimacy cannot endure. Lamps without oil flicker out when the midnight cry comes.

And what is the oil? It is not talent or zeal or religious effort. It is intimacy—the overflow of communion with the Father. It is the fragrance of belonging, pressed from the olives of rest. It is what burns in hearts that have stopped striving and started abiding.

In this hour, the Spirit is crying out: "Do not run dry." A Church busy with programs but barren of presence will falter in the darkness. A generation filled with noise but void of oil will burn out before the dawn. But a people resting in the

Father's embrace—receiving His delight, drinking deeply of His love—will shine like torches in the night.

Rest is not weakness. Rest is oil.

Every time you resist the urge to perform and choose instead to sit at His feet, your jar fills. Every moment you trade noise for nearness, your flame grows stronger. Every surrender becomes a drop of oil that the enemy cannot steal.

The billion-soul harvest will not be carried by the exhausted, but by the anointed—by sons and daughters who burn with the steady flame of intimacy. They will not need to announce revival; they will carry it in their eyes. When they walk into classrooms, boardrooms, studios, and streets, atmospheres will shift. The world will know they have been with Jesus.

This is the mystery of divine exchange: orphans strive for power, but sons and daughters receive oil. Striving demands more effort; intimacy releases more presence. And when you rest in love, the flame burns brighter because it's fueled by grace, not grit.

I've seen glimpses of it—the quiet revivals that begin not with noise, but with stillness. A few believers gathered around a kitchen table, not to perform, but to adore. No microphones, no agendas—just tears, laughter, and worship rising from hearts at rest. And suddenly, the air shifts. The oil begins to flow. Peace fills the room like a weighty fragrance, and chains of anxiety break without a word being spoken.

That is revival in its truest form: not something you host, but Someone you welcome.

And this oil—it's costly. You cannot borrow it from another's encounter. You cannot purchase it with performance. It is formed in the secret place, pressed in the stillness, refined in surrender. When you close the door, silence the scroll, and let the Father sing over you, the crushing becomes anointing and intimacy becomes fire.

Zephaniah 3:17 is not poetic sentiment—it is the furnace of revival itself: *"He will rejoice over you with gladness; He will quiet you by His love; He will exult over you with loud singing."*

That song fills your jar. That song keeps your lamp burning when the night grows long. That song steadies your hands when the Bridegroom delays.

Beloved, the harvest will not come through noise, but through oil. The Bride will not be ready by busyness, but by belonging. And belonging begins with rest. Every "yes" to His embrace becomes a flame. Every Sabbath of the soul becomes a declaration: Babylon is not my master; my Father is my source.

This is the Father's strategy for revival: not louder, but deeper. Not faster, but fuller. Not striving, but resting. A Bride who has ceased performing and begun abiding. A people whose lamps are trimmed, whose jars are overflowing, whose hearts burn with the oil of divine love.

The Father's love is the oil that will carry the Church through the midnight hour and light the way for the greatest harvest in history. And it begins right here—with you—choosing rest as rebellion, letting His delight fill your jar until the nations see the flame and run toward the light.

The King is coming. The cry is near.

And the oil of His love is the only fire that will last.

Finding Home in His Love

The Father's love is not theory—it's encounter. It meets us where words run out and hearts grow weary. For many, it comes not in moments of triumph but in seasons of waiting—when promises feel delayed, when relationships fracture, when prayers seem to echo unanswered.

Waiting has a way of exposing the orphan lie that whispers, "You've failed. You're forgotten. You'll never be whole again." But that is where the Father comes running. Not with explanations. Not with conditions. Just with love. His presence wraps around the weary like the robe on the prodigal's shoulders. His whisper becomes oil to the soul: *"You are Mine. You are still My child. You are still My beloved. Nothing and no one can take that away."*

That whisper changes everything. It quiets striving and rewrites identity. It turns disappointment into intercession, longing into legacy. Every wound becomes a well for compassion. Every unanswered prayer becomes a seed for future harvest. The waiting is not wasted—it's where oil is formed.

Many of us carry prayers that have not yet been answered—names we lift daily, dreams that still sleep beneath the soil, stories that haven't yet turned toward redemption. But the Father's running heart is toward all of it. His love is not limited by distance or time. His arms reach farther than regret. His song is stronger than silence.

And so, we keep writing. We keep praying. We keep believing. Not from striving, but from rest. Every word of faith, every whispered "yes," every prayer lifted in trust becomes oil poured before the Lord. None of it is wasted. Every drop counts.

Rest is not pretending the ache isn't real—it's handing the ache back to Abba and letting Him sing over it. Rest is not a pause from battle; it is the posture of victory. It is how sons and daughters learn to live above the sun—held, known, and secure in perfect love.

And in that place of stillness, something begins to shift. The same love that comforts you starts to commission you. The peace that quiets your soul begins to burn as holy fire. Rest becomes revelation: that every burden you surrender becomes oil, and every delay you entrust becomes destiny. What looks like stillness on the surface is actually alignment underneath—heaven preparing you for what's ahead.

You begin to realize that the waiting has been forming endurance, that the silence has been training your ears, and that the ache itself has become a vessel for glory. Rest does not leave you idle; it roots you deeper in love so you can stand unshaken when the shaking comes.

This is the mystery of His embrace: it satisfies the soul today and carries the promise of tomorrow. It is both sanctuary and sending place—the Father's table and the Father's commission.

So we rest.

We trust.

We wait.

And in the waiting, the oil flows.

Because from this stillness comes the next sound—the prophetic call to rest. Not the rest of retreat, but the rest of resistance. Not escape, but empowerment. The Father is teaching His sons and daughters to war from peace, to carry authority from intimacy, and to shift nations from the quiet place of His love.

The Prophetic Call to Rest

The oil that flows from stillness is not meant to remain contained—it becomes a sound. A summons. A prophetic call. When sons and daughters rediscover the rest of the Father, heaven releases a new rhythm into the earth. This rhythm defies Babylon's demands and dismantles the world's machinery of performance. It is the sound of freedom, the cadence of belonging, the heartbeat of revival.

Rest is not weakness—it is warfare. It is rebellion against a culture addicted to proving itself. When you choose to rest in the Father's love, you are declaring to every power of darkness: *I already belong. I am already loved. I am already secure in Him.* That declaration shakes the kingdom of fear because it strips the enemy of his favorite leverage—striving, shame, and self-reliance.

Striving is slavery; rest is freedom. Striving is the orphan's cry; rest is the son's song. Striving bows to the culture of achievement; rest bows to the King who runs. And in that bowing, authority is born.

Think of Israel in Egypt. Pharaoh's whip demanded endless labor—make more bricks with less straw. That's the world's system: do more, prove more, earn more. And what was God's answer? A command to stop. The Sabbath was not about leisure; it was a declaration of deliverance. Every day they rested, Israel was prophesying, *Pharaoh no longer rules me. Yahweh is my Source.*

The same call resounds now. The spirit of Pharaoh has not died; it just wears new clothes—schedules, metrics, algorithms, and unending noise. It drives humanity to exhaustion, convincing us that if we stop, everything will collapse. But heaven whispers otherwise: *"Be still and know that I am God."* (Psalm 46:10)

This is why the enemy hates rest—because when you rest, you break his system. You stop feeding the lie that worth comes from work. You silence the noise that tries to define you. You return to divine order, where the soul no longer leads, the body no longer drives, and the spirit—alive with Holy Spirit— takes its rightful place at the helm.

In rest, you see clearly again. You remember who you are and whose you are. You trade the language of scarcity for the song of sufficiency. You stop trying to hold everything together and discover that the Father already is.

I sense Holy Spirit speaking even now: *"My people must learn to rest, or they will be crushed under the weight of this age. Those who rest in My love will stand when others fall. Those who rest in My embrace will carry oil when lamps go dark. Those who rest in My delight will shine as My Bride, ready for My return."*

This is not the hour to collapse from exhaustion—it is the hour to resist exhaustion with the rhythm of heaven. Rest is not retreat; it is strategy. It is the fireproofing of your faith. It is how the Bride prepares for the Bridegroom.

So pause here, beloved. Take a breath. Ask yourself quietly:

Where am I still striving for what has already been given?

Where have I allowed Pharaoh's whip to replace the Father's song?

Where have I confused movement with fruitfulness, and noise with life?

The prophetic call to rest is not an invitation to laziness—it is a call to alignment. It is the Father's strategy for the days ahead. It is how His sons and daughters will carry revival without being consumed by it.

Lay down the whip. Receive the robe. Cease striving, and step into your inheritance. Rest as resistance. Rest as worship. Rest as warfare. Because in the end, it will not be the restless who rebuild the ruins of this generation, but the resting—those who have learned to live from the Father's love and pour its oil into a weary world.

A Vision for a Resting Generation

I can see them—clear as dawn over a quiet sea—a generation learning to live from rest in a restless world. They are sons and daughters who no longer bow to Pharaoh's whip of performance or Babylon's lure of comparison. Their worth is not measured in output, visibility, or applause. They have found a deeper rhythm—the rhythm of the Father's heart.

While the world scrolls itself into exhaustion, they carry oil— the oil of intimacy, the oil of adoption, the oil of belonging. Their lamps do not flicker when others fade, because their secret is not their hustle but their home. They have discovered that stillness is not stagnation but strength, and that peace is not the absence of conflict but the presence of the King.

This resting generation will not be loud in flesh but radiant in Spirit. Their quietness will break atmospheres. Their calm will confound chaos. Their joy will disarm despair. They will move through cities, campuses, and nations as carriers of an unseen kingdom—anchored, unhurried, aflame.

I see glimpses of them everywhere:

• Students fasting not for popularity but for purity, their surrendered hearts turning classrooms into prayer rooms.

• Parents transforming dinner tables into altars, blessing their children until anxiety bows to peace.

• Pastors trading ambition for intimacy, shepherding not by pressure but by presence.

• Elders and intercessors who may never hold microphones but hold nations in prayer, their stillness shaking the heavens.

They are not defined by noise; they are marked by nearness. They are not driven by outcomes; they are drawn by love. Their rest is their rebellion, their stillness their strategy, their peace their prophetic weapon.

This is the generation that will carry the billion-soul harvest—not through burnout but through belovedness. They will not run on adrenaline but on oil. Their authority will not come from platforms but from prayer. And when the midnight cry comes, their lamps will already be burning.

Listen—the Spirit is speaking over them even now: *"I am raising up a resting remnant. They will walk in peace that disarms chaos, in joy that defies despair, and in rest that becomes the roar of revival. They will not merely survive the shaking—they will steady it with My presence."*

This is the vision of the Father's heart—a generation of sons and daughters who live above the sun, carrying the fragrance of His delight into every dark place. They are not many, but they are enough. They are not frantic, but they are fierce in love.

And you, reader, are part of them. The invitation is not distant; it is here, now. The Father is calling you into the same rhythm—into holy rest that becomes holy fire. Sit in His presence until the striving breaks. Let His love fill your jar until peace spills over every boundary of your life.

Because the world will not be changed by exhausted laborers, but by resting lovers.

For Today: A Prophetic Invitation to Rest

The Father's arms are open now—wide, unwavering, and waiting. This is not theory, not poetry, not wishful thinking. It is invitation. The kind that carries weight in heaven. The kind that rearranges everything when you say yes.

The world will keep pulling you toward its cycle of exhaustion—its endless notifications, its ceaseless comparisons, its demand to prove yourself. But over that noise comes a gentler voice, the sound that started it all: *"Come to Me, all who labor and are heavy laden, and I will give you rest."* (Matthew 11:28)

Rest is not retreat. It is resistance. It is warfare waged in silence against the systems that scream for your attention. Every time you choose rest, you break an agreement with fear. Every time you pause to listen for His heartbeat, you overthrow another idol of productivity.

- Rest says, I am not what I produce.
- Rest says, I am loved even when I am unseen.
- Rest says, I am secure because He sings over me.

This is not a passive stillness—it's a prophetic stand. The kind that confronts darkness not with striving, but with peace. The kind that terrifies the enemy because peace cannot be manipulated and love cannot be bought.

Here's what I sense the Father inviting you to do:

• Lay down performance. Stop measuring your worth by activity or applause. You are already accepted.

• Listen for His song. Let Zephaniah 3:17 wash over you until His delight becomes your atmosphere.

• Cry, "Abba." Let Romans 8:15 reshape your prayers—not as a servant pleading for favor, but as a child resting in love.

• Choose rest as warfare. Each time you reject the lie that you must earn His affection, heaven shakes, and hell loses ground.

Then pause. Breathe. Whisper His name. Let silence become your sanctuary.

Prayer

Abba, I come to You now.

I lay down my striving, my fear, my need to prove, and I rest in Your love.

Place Your robe upon my shoulders, Your ring upon my hand, Your sandals upon my feet.

Quiet my soul with Your song.

Let Your peace disarm every storm, and let Your joy become my strength.

Teach me to live from Your delight, to move at the pace of Your presence, to carry Your love as oil for this generation.

Let my rest become resistance, my stillness a sanctuary, and my life a lamp that burns until the Bridegroom comes.

I am Yours. Completely. Forever. Amen.

Beloved, this is your moment.

Not tomorrow. Not someday. Now.

This is your Esther courage, your Joseph endurance, your Bride's invitation—to live as one wholly loved, fully known, entirely at rest.

The Father is not calling you to prove your devotion.

He's calling you to dwell in His delight.

This is the rest that fuels revival, the oil that keeps the flame alive, the secret place that no storm can steal.

Rest is not denial; it's where we learn to carry pain without losing our seat.

So exhale. Be still. Receive His love.

The King is coming.

And the oil of His rest will be the fire that lights the way.

Chapter 8 — Grief, Boundaries, and Living Above the Sun

Living above the sun does not mean living untouched by loss. It does not mean bypassing sorrow, silencing ache, or pretending that love has not been interrupted.

It means learning how to carry grief without letting it govern you. It means setting boundaries without surrendering love. It means remaining seated with Christ while unresolved relationships still exist on the earth.

This chapter is about learning how to grieve from the Spirit—not from the wound.

There are seasons when living above the sun feels spacious and light. And then there are seasons when it feels costly—quietly costly.

This is a chapter for those seasons.

Grief Below the Sun and Grief Above the Sun

Below the sun, grief demands answers.

It asks: Why did this happen? How do I fix it? When will this resolve? What do I need to do to feel whole again?

Below the sun, grief is measured by outcomes—by reconciliation, by apology, by restoration that can be seen, named, and completed.

And when those outcomes do not come, grief below the sun begins to harden. It turns inward. It becomes self-protective. It begins to shape identity.

Above the sun, grief is not resolved—it is entrusted.

It is carried into the presence of God and governed by truth rather than circumstance. It is held without being explained. It is acknowledged without being obeyed.

Above-the-sun grief says:

I feel the ache—but it does not define me. I do not deny the loss—but I refuse to live beneath it. I am seated with Christ even while my heart still aches.

This is not spiritual bypassing. This is spiritual alignment.

Grief acknowledged below the sun can harden the heart. Grief surrendered above the sun softens it.

The pain may remain—but it no longer determines posture.

Boundaries Are Not Rejection — They Are Stewardship

One of the great confusions in modern Christian culture is the belief that love requires access. It does not.

Jesus loved perfectly—and still withdrew. He forgave freely—and still entrusted Himself to the Father, not to people. He remained open-hearted without remaining endlessly available. Boundaries are not walls of bitterness. They are guardrails of wisdom. They do not exist to punish others. They exist to steward the heart.

Living above the sun teaches us that: You can love without proximity. You can forgive without reconciliation. You can honor without agreement.

Boundaries built below the sun are often constructed from fear—fear of being hurt again, fear of conflict, fear of loss. Boundaries built above the sun are formed from clarity—clarity of calling, clarity of conscience, clarity of peace.

They protect the heart without closing it. They allow love to remain clean.

When Separation Was Not Your Choice

There is a distinct grief reserved for those who did not choose the distance.

It comes when family narratives quietly shift, when accusations replace conversation, when silence replaces relationship. This grief is heavier because it carries powerlessness. There is no conversation to have. No misunderstanding to clarify. No door you are allowed to knock on.

And in that space, many believers exhaust themselves trying to repair what they did not rupture—carrying responsibility that was never assigned to them by God.

Living above the sun does not demand that you fix what you did not break. It teaches you to release responsibility for outcomes you do not control.

This is not resignation.
It is surrender.

Above-the-sun living whispers: *You are not required to carry what was never yours to hold.* There is a holy release in that truth.

Bearing With One Another — Without Losing Yourself

Scripture calls us to bear with one another in love. It does not call us to dissolve ourselves in the process. Bearing with does not mean enduring manipulation. It does not mean tolerating abuse. It does not mean abandoning truth for the sake of peace.

It means remaining governed by the Spirit while others remain governed by fear, pain, or deception.

This is the narrow way.

It is possible to keep your heart soft, your boundaries firm, your posture humble, and your conscience clear. This is not weakness. This is maturity. This is living above the sun.

Jesus: The Model of Unresolved Love

Jesus lived with unresolved relationships. His own family misunderstood Him. His disciples abandoned Him. Religious leaders falsely accused Him.

Yet He did not harden. He did not retaliate. He did not force reconciliation. He entrusted Himself to the Father. He loved without demand. He spoke truth without compulsion. He walked in peace without insisting on agreement.

Living above the sun means following Jesus not only in power—but in posture. Not only in miracles—but in meekness.

A Stillness Pause

Before moving on, allow yourself to stop for a moment. You do not need to resolve anything here. You do not need to revisit the story. You do not need to reach a conclusion.

Simply notice where you are seated.

Notice what you are carrying. Notice what feels heavy—and what no longer needs to be. Let what is unresolved remain with God. Let what is painful be held by Him. Remain where you are—in Christ.

The Invitation: To Grieve Without Losing Your Seat

This chapter invites you to pause and ask—not urgently, not defensively, but honestly: Where am I carrying grief from below the sun? Where am I allowing pain to dictate my posture? Where is God inviting me to remain seated—even while my heart still aches?

Living above the sun does not promise resolution. It promises alignment. And alignment is where peace is found.

Closing Truth

You are not failing because it still hurts.
You are not faithless because it remains unresolved.

You are learning how to grieve without descending.
You are learning how to love without losing yourself.
You are learning how to remain seated while the earth remains unfinished.

You are learning how to live above the sun.

When God Breathes Life Back Into the Body

Grief does not only live in memory or emotion—it settles quietly into the body. Long after the soul has chosen truth and the spirit has found its footing above the sun, the body often continues to carry what was never fully released.

Tension, fatigue, shallow breathing, and weariness are not signs of spiritual failure; they are evidence of a heart that has endured deeply.

Scripture reminds us that we were not created as divided beings. God formed us as spirit, soul, and body—each meant to be held, restored, and aligned by His presence. And just as truth renews the mind and hope steadies the soul, God also restores the body through the most intimate and overlooked gift He has given us: breath.

Before we learn to walk forward in daily communion, we must first allow the Lord to breathe life back into the places where grief has taken residence. This is not striving. It is not technique. It is a return to the way God first gave us life—by breathing Himself into us.

What follows is an invitation to slow down, to receive, and to let the God who formed you also re-form you—one breath at a time.

There are seasons when the Lord heals the soul first, and the body lags behind—not because the body is rebellious, but because it has learned survival.

Trauma teaches the body to brace. Grief teaches it to tighten.
Long seasons of pressure teach it to stay alert even when the danger has passed.

And yet, from the beginning, God designed the human body not for vigilance, but for **communion**.

"Then the Lord God formed the man of dust from the ground and breathed into his nostrils the breath of life." (Genesis 2:7)

Notice the order. Before Adam worked. Before he spoke. Before he named anything. He breathed.

Life did not enter humanity through striving or obedience. Life entered through **divine breath**.

This means something essential: **The body was designed to live by receiving, not by performing.**

The Body Carries What the Soul Endures

Many believers learn how to endure spiritually while their bodies quietly absorb the cost.

Years of betrayal. Years of loss. Years of misunderstanding. Years of carrying what should have been shared.

Scripture never shames the body for this. *"My frame was not hidden from you, when I was being made in secret."* (Psalm 139:15)

God sees the frame. He knows the nervous system. He understands how grief settles into muscles and joints.

Healing, then, is not God "fixing" a failure. It is God **re-introducing safety**.

This is why Jesus often healed people before they understood theology. Their bodies responded to presence before their minds could explain it.

Breath Is Where Healing Begins

Breath is the meeting place of heaven and earth inside the human body. *"The Spirit of God has made me, and the breath of the Almighty gives me life."* (Job 33:4)

When we breathe slowly and intentionally, we are not creating life—we are **agreeing with it.**

The name of God—YHWH—cannot be spoken without breath. It is inhaled and exhaled. Every breath becomes a quiet confession: He is here. He sustains me. I am not alone.

A Guided Prayer of Alignment Through Breath

This is not a ritual. It is remembrance. Sit comfortably. Place one hand on your chest, one on your abdomen.

Step 1: Receiving

Inhale slowly through your nose. As you breathe in, pray quietly: "You breathed life into me."

Pause briefly—not holding, just resting.

Step 2: Releasing

Exhale gently through your mouth. As you breathe out, pray:

"I release what my body has been carrying."

Let your shoulders drop. Let the jaw soften.

"Cast your burden on the Lord, and He will sustain you." (Psalm 55:22) Repeat this rhythm several times.

Speaking Peace to the Body

Jesus did not only speak to storms outside of people. He spoke peace into chaos wherever it appeared.

"Peace, be still." (Mark 4:39)

You are allowed to speak this same peace **to your own body**.

Quietly, without force, say:

- *Body, you are safe in Christ.*

- *Body, you are no longer required to brace.*

- *Body, come into alignment with the life of Jesus within me.*

"The life I now live in the body, I live by faith in the Son of God." (Galatians 2:20)

This is not self-soothing divorced from faith. This is faith applied to the whole person.

Healing Is Alignment, Not Effort

Many people believe healing requires intensity. Scripture reveals it requires agreement.

"If the Spirit of Him who raised Jesus from the dead dwells in you, He will also give life to your mortal bodies." (Romans 8:11)

Life flows where resistance ends. The body does not need to be convinced—it needs permission to rest. And rest is not passivity. Rest is **trust embodied**.

Living Above the Sun Includes the Body

To live above the sun is to allow heaven to govern every layer of existence. Spirit first. Then soul. Then body.

When the spirit is at rest in God, the soul settles. When the soul settles, the body follows. This is why Jesus often said, *"Your faith has made you well."* Faith is alignment with reality as God defines it. The body heals best when it knows it is no longer alone.

A Closing Breath-Prayer of Consecration

Inhale: *"In Him I live."*

Exhale: *"And move and have my being."* (Acts 17:28)

Sit in silence for a moment. Let the breath preach what words cannot.

Short Devotional Version - Breathing Life in a Season of Grief

When grief is long and answers are few, the body often carries what the heart cannot say. Scripture reminds us that life itself entered humanity through God's breath—not through striving, understanding, or strength.

Today, you do not need to fix anything. Sit quietly. Breathe slowly. Let each breath remind you that God is still giving life. *"The Lord is near to the brokenhearted."* (Psalm 34:18)

As you inhale, receive His nearness. As you exhale, release what you cannot carry. Healing does not always come as a moment. Sometimes it comes as permission to rest. And even here, God is faithful.

Chapter 9 — Walking in Daily Communion

The Introduction: The River's Edge

Come with me to the river's edge. Not a dry streamed that speaks of what once was, nor a flash flood that comes and goes, but a steady current—clear, alive, flowing from the throne of God (Revelation 22:1). Listen closely. Its rhythm is louder than your thoughts yet gentler than your fears. The world behind you still hums with noise—notifications, deadlines, expectations—but here the river silences them all. Its waters are cool against your feet, inviting you to step deeper, to be carried where your own strength never could.

This river is communion. Not ritual. Not religion. Not a spiritual "check-in." It is the unbroken flow of His presence moving through your every moment—shaping decisions, carrying burdens, saturating silence. To walk in daily communion is to live inside that flow, where your breath and His breath intertwine, where movement and stillness become one.

Communion is how we keep grieving hearts from drifting below the sun.

This is what Paul meant when he declared, *"In Him we live and move and have our being"* (Acts 17:28). Notice the order—it begins in Him, not outside striving to get in. You are not a body chasing spiritual experiences or a soul grasping for identity. You are first a spirit—awakened by Christ, designed to walk in rhythm with Holy Spirit (Galatians 5:25). You are a spirit being, that has a soul, that lives in a body. When your spirit leads—anchored in communion—your soul aligns, your body follows, and your whole life becomes a living river in a desert world.

Daily communion is not a luxury for the spiritually mature; it is survival for the sons and daughters of this hour. It is the oil for your lamp when others run dry. It is the flame that will not flicker when the world grows cold. Joseph endured because of it. Esther found courage because of it. Every act of obedience in their lives was born from intimacy—and yours will be too.

Many try to live off moments—Sunday highs, worship nights, brief devotionals squeezed between responsibilities—only to find themselves parched by Monday morning. That's like sipping from a cup while the river roars beside you. The invitation of the Spirit is not to moments only, but to the flow. Communion is not about dipping your toes—it's about surrendering to the current until His rhythm becomes your own.

This is what Jesus described when He said, *"Abide in Me, and I in you. As the branch cannot bear fruit by itself, unless it abides in the vine, neither can you, unless you abide in Me"* (John 15:4). Abide. Stay. Remain. Communion is not a visit—it is a dwelling.

And here is the wonder: this dwelling is not labor; it is rest. The Father's love has already run toward us—clothing us, quieting our striving, restoring our song. We have learned how to remain seated with Christ even when the earth still feels unfinished, how to carry grief without descending, and how to steward love with wisdom. Now, we step into the daily river that sustains that posture—communion that becomes rhythm, breath, and life.

The world will still tempt you with its counterfeit currents—scrolls of distraction, cycles of performance, storms of fear. But daily communion is rebellion against all of it. Each whisper of His name is a declaration: *"My source is not under the sun. My source is above it."* Every time you choose stillness over noise, Scripture over scroll, presence over pressure, you're anchoring your feet in the river that never runs dry.

This is the invitation: step to the river's edge, and do not stop there. Step in. Let the current carry you. For communion is not something you schedule—it is Someone you walk with. And that Someone has promised: *"I am with you always, to the end of the age"* (Matthew 28:20).

The Flow of Communion: A Life with God

The river you've stepped into is not seasonal. It is not a burst of emotion or a weekend encounter that fades by Monday morning. It is steady—eternal—flowing from the heart of the Father through every moment of your life. You can feel its consistency, like breath, like heartbeat. That is communion: not a rhythm you perform, but a rhythm you return to, again and again, until your life moves as one with His.

Jesus painted this reality with the image of a vineyard:

"Abide in Me, and I in you. As the branch cannot bear fruit by itself, unless it abides in the vine, neither can you, unless you abide in Me. I am the vine; you are the branches. Whoever abides in Me and I in him, he it is that bears much fruit, for apart from Me you can do nothing." (John 15:4–5)

225 | P a g e

The branch doesn't strain to produce. It simply stays connected. The life of the vine flows naturally, quietly, faithfully through it until fruit appears. That is the flow of communion—His life in you, your life in Him. No striving. No scrambling. Just union. You don't live off borrowed water, rationing drops of revelation. You live from the stream itself.

I've known both ways. There were seasons when I treated communion like an appointment—a task I could check off before rushing into the day. I would show up, drink deeply for a moment, and wonder why I was dry again by nightfall. But then Holy Spirit whispered: *"You were never meant to sip from a cup. You were meant to live in the river."*

That changed everything. I stopped visiting God and started walking with Him. I realized communion is not about getting filled—it's about staying connected. It's not about feeling something; it's about abiding in Someone.

This is how Jesus lived. Crowds pressed in, storms raged around Him, accusations followed Him—but He never lost peace. Why? Because He never left the flow. *"I am in the Father, and the Father is in Me"* (John 14:11). Every word He spoke, every miracle He performed, every step He took flowed out of intimacy. He didn't hustle for God's presence; He carried it.

And this is your invitation—not to moments of inspiration, but to a lifestyle of abiding. Imagine your day if His presence became the air you breathed, not the appointment you rushed through. Imagine decisions shaped by His peace, conversations softened by His kindness, rest defined by His nearness. That's not a fantasy. That's the fruit of communion.

The river beneath your life doesn't demand noise or performance—it requires connection. The secret isn't trying harder; it's staying longer. Abide. Stay. Dwell. The longer you remain, the steadier the flow becomes, and the less the storms can shake you.

Joseph's endurance flowed from this river. Esther's courage was born in it. David's worship rose from it. Jesus' ministry was sustained by it. And your calling—whatever it may look like—will only endure through it.

The flow of communion is not reserved for a few; it is the inheritance of every son and daughter. You were never meant to live parched, running from one spiritual oasis to the next. You were created to live submerged—to let His current carry you, to let His voice define you, to let His presence become your atmosphere.

Remain in the flow. The fruit will come.

Enoch: Walking With God

If the river of communion had a name in Scripture, one of them would be Enoch. In just a few words, the Bible sums up his entire life: *"Enoch walked with God, and he was not, for God took him."* (Genesis 5:24)

No recorded sermons.

No grand achievements.

No crowds, no accolades, no monuments.

Just this: he walked with God.

Day after day, step by step, in a rhythm of nearness that made heaven long to bring him home.

Enoch lived in one of the darkest eras recorded in Genesis—a time of violence, corruption, and decay so deep that judgment would soon come through the flood. Yet while the world around him drowned in chaos, Enoch found a current stronger than the culture. He chose intimacy when everyone else chose noise. His quiet walk became a prophetic act of defiance against the age he lived in.

That's the power of obscurity. Hidden seasons may look small to the world, but they echo loudly in heaven. Enoch's greatness wasn't measured by visibility—it was measured by proximity. Every unseen prayer, every private conversation with God, every step taken in secret fellowship was counted as friendship in eternity.

There is something holy about lives that vanish into the presence of God. Enoch didn't "disappear" in the sense of escape—he simply became more at home in heaven than on earth. His walk grew so close that the veil between realms grew thin until it could no longer hold him. That is what communion does: it blurs the line between here and there, between time and eternity.

I have often pondered what those walks must have been like—mornings filled with quiet listening, evenings lit by the glow of conversation, ordinary days marked by extraordinary awareness. Enoch wasn't chasing encounters; he was cultivating presence. He wasn't striving to be seen; he was learning to stay. That is the essence of daily communion: to remain where He is until the world no longer pulls stronger than His nearness.

Maybe that's the hidden secret of revival—it doesn't begin with microphones, but with footsteps. With people who walk when no one's watching. With hearts that choose nearness over notoriety.

Enoch's story tells us that heaven values friendship over fame. God is not impressed by our platforms; He's moved by our presence. Revival history is written by those who walked with Him in hidden fields long before their names were ever known.

So let this encourage you: the prayers you whisper when no one notices, the tears you shed where no one applauds, the obedience you offer when no one affirms—these are not wasted. They are the quiet steps of communion. Heaven is recording them.

To walk with God is not to escape the world; it is to bring heaven's rhythm into it. Every faithful step, every surrendered moment, every unseen act of love leaves footprints of glory in the dust of this earth.

This is what communion looks like when it matures—not a single moment of encounter, but a life of continual awareness. A life where you and God move together until His steps become your own.

What if that is what He is inviting you into today? Not a race. Not a ritual. Just a walk. One step at a time. One whisper at a time. One breath at a time.

Until one day, like Enoch, you are found no more—because you have finally become what you were always meant to be: one with Him.

Mary of Bethany: Sitting at His Feet

If Enoch shows us the beauty of walking with God, Mary of Bethany reveals the wonder of stopping with Him.

Where Enoch walked, Mary sat.

Where the world hurried, she lingered.

And in her stillness, the heart of Jesus found rest.

Luke paints the moment with quiet simplicity: Martha welcomed Him into her house… and she had a sister called Mary, who sat at the Lord's feet and listened to His teaching. But Martha was distracted with much serving… And the Lord answered her, *"Martha, Martha, you are anxious and troubled about many things, but one thing is necessary. Mary has chosen the good portion, which will not be taken away from her."* (Luke 10:38–42)

One thing. Not ten tasks. Not endless doing. One thing—His presence.

Martha's house could be any of ours—busy, demanding, full of good intentions but frantic energy. Her service wasn't wrong, but her pace was misaligned. She welcomed Jesus into her home, yet missed the invitation to sit at His feet. Mary, on the other hand, discerned the moment. She knew that the meal could wait, but the presence could not.

This is the tension every believer faces in an age of hurry: doing for God versus being with God. Martha's posture builds the kitchen; Mary's posture fills the room with fragrance. Martha manages; Mary ministers. And Jesus still calls her choice *"the good portion."*

Mary's sitting was not passivity—it was holy defiance. In a world that celebrates busyness, she dared to be still. Her silence became her statement: *"I will not be defined by my productivity. I will be defined by His voice."*

The same Spirit is whispering this call again. Our generation wears exhaustion like honor, believing that movement equals meaning. Yet the One we serve keeps pointing to a different rhythm—less rush, more rest; less noise, more knowing.

I know this tension well. There have been Martha days when my calendar was full but my heart was empty—when I worked hard for God yet felt far from Him. But in every season, He has gently called me back to Mary's posture: *"Come, sit at My feet again."* And when I do, something holy happens. The noise recedes. The pressure dissolves. His presence begins to reorder everything inside me.

Mary's story is a prophetic mirror for the modern Church. We have built programs and platforms, filled schedules and sound systems—but what Jesus desires most is simple: communion. Revival will not come from busyness, but from being. The oil of intimacy is never poured out in the kitchen of chaos; it flows in the posture of devotion.

Imagine what could happen if a generation chose Mary's portion. If students closed their screens to listen. If parents

231 | Page

turned their tables into altars. If leaders paused meetings to wait on His whisper. If churches traded agendas for adoration.

That's where transformation begins—in the stillness of hearts that refuse to hurry past His presence. Mary's portion cannot be taken because it was never earned. It was received. And everything else—status, success, noise—will fade away, but what we receive at His feet will remain forever.

So pause for a moment. Let the dishes wait. Let the world spin without you for a breath. He is in the room. Sit. Listen. And know that the "one thing" is enough.

The War for Communion in These Days

Mary's quiet posture in a noisy house wasn't just devotion—it was defiance. Her stillness was war. And the same war rages now.

We live in an age where noise is worshiped and distraction is weaponized. The world no longer rests—it performs, scrolls, reacts, and consumes. Attention has become the most valuable currency on earth, and the enemy has learned to spend it well. His goal isn't simply to tempt you with sin; it's to drown you in static until the whisper of God can no longer be heard.

That's the real battle for this generation: not unbelief, but unbroken distraction.

We are living in a modern Martha world, where hurry has become holy and noise feels like necessity. Notifications call louder than prayer. The feed outpaces the Word. Even in ministry, the temptation to perform has replaced the invitation to abide. And all the while, the still, small voice of the Spirit is whispering, *"Be still and know that I am God."* (Psalm 46:10)

The war for communion is not subtle—it is spiritual. It is the enemy's oldest strategy cloaked in modern form. In Eden, it began with a whisper that replaced truth. In Babylon, it became the hum of endless labor. Today, it wears the glow of a screen and the pulse of hurry. The result is the same: hearts that no longer hear.

And yet, in the midst of this noise, the Spirit is raising up a different kind of people—those who refuse to trade presence for productivity, or truth for trends. They are learning that stillness is not passivity; it is resistance. Silence is not emptiness; it is alignment. Every time they stop to listen, they are waging war against a culture that profits from their distraction.

You may recognize the moment when believers make this choice—when worry is exchanged for worship, reaction yields to prayer, and pressure gives way to adoration. Peace begins to govern where fear once ruled. Wisdom rises where anxiety once dictated decisions. Hearts soften, homes steady, and spiritual authority strengthens—not through striving, but through surrender.

This is how transformation often unfolds. Not loudly. Not instantly. But faithfully—when the heart turns toward God instead of turning inward. What begins as a quiet decision becomes a shift in atmosphere, and alignment releases fruit that could never be produced by force.

This is what the war for communion looks like: not louder, but deeper. Not more activity, but more awareness.

Cancel culture, comparison culture, hustle culture—they are all branches of the same ancient tree: Babel reborn, man's attempt to reach heaven by his own noise. But communion is Heaven's counterculture. Every time you choose His presence over performance, you are tearing down towers built on pride. Every pause, every prayer, every whispered "Jesus" is warfare that shifts atmospheres.

This is why communion cannot be reduced to a ritual—it is a revolution. The one who abides becomes unshakable because he lives from a different source. Esther could fast because she trusted love more than fear. Joseph could endure prison because he carried presence more than pain. And you—you will stand in this hour only if your roots reach the river.

The war is real, but the victory is already written. The enemy cannot outshout the whisper of God, and he cannot outlast the peace that flows from His presence.

So choose your side each day. The world will always call you back to the kitchen of hurry. The Spirit will always invite you to the feet of communion. One leads to burnout; the other to burning. One drains; the other fills. One exhausts; the other ignites.

The invitation remains the same as it was in Mary's house: "One thing is necessary."

In this hour of shaking, may that one thing become your everything.

The Practice of Daily Communion

If communion is war, then your daily rhythms are your weapons. Not the heavy weapons of human effort, but the light and effortless tools of love—simple acts that tether your heart to heaven in a world that's constantly pulling you away.

Communion isn't a rigid schedule; it's a living rhythm. It's not what you do for God—it's what you do with Him. Every small yes to His presence becomes a strike against the noise of Babylon. Every pause, every prayer, every whispered worship reclaims territory in your soul.

Start your day with His voice. Before headlines, before messages, before the world's noise, open His Word. Let Scripture be the first sound your spirit hears. Even a single verse—breathed slowly, listened to deeply—can set the tone for your day. It's not how much you read, but who you meet in the reading. That's where communion begins.

Pause in the storm. Life won't stop pressing—emails, conflict, temptation, fatigue. But communion isn't destroyed by chaos; it's revealed in it. When you pause, even for thirty seconds, and whisper, *"Speak, Lord, Your servant is listening,"* (1 Samuel 3:10) you realign heaven and earth within you. In that stillness, strongholds lose power. The storm doesn't always change—but you do.

Worship in the flow. Communion isn't confined to your prayer room. It spills into the kitchen, the commute, the hallway, the office. A quiet song under your breath, a psalm spoken aloud, a moment of gratitude between tasks—these are altar fires that sanctify your day. Remember Paul and Silas in prison: their midnight worship wasn't a performance, it was a declaration—and the earth shook (Acts 16:25–26).

Journal His whispers. Write what He says, even if it's just a sentence or a fragment. Journaling isn't busywork—it's testimony-building. It transforms fleeting impressions into anchors of remembrance. Over time, those pages become scrolls of His faithfulness, proof that He was speaking all along. What you record today may sustain you—or your children—years from now.

Walk with Him in creation. Sometimes the holiest thing you can do is step outside. Breathe. Look up. Watch the sky move, the leaves sway, the light shift. Romans 1:20 says His invisible qualities are revealed in what He has made. Creation becomes a cathedral when you slow down enough to notice. When you whisper, "Thank You," to the wind, it carries your worship into eternity.

Fast as resistance. Fasting isn't punishment—it's recalibration. It's your spirit saying to your flesh, "You're not in charge." When you fast, you quiet appetites that compete with hunger for God. In a culture addicted to indulgence, fasting is rebellion wrapped in devotion. It turns craving into communion, emptiness into encounter.

These rhythms are not chores; they're lifelines. They keep you anchored when life pulls hard. They're not about performing for God—they're about staying aware of Him. Every rhythm is a reminder: you are not living from the world up—you are living from heaven down.

And as you practice communion, you begin to notice the shift. The days no longer feel fragmented—they begin to flow. Your work becomes worship. Your conversations become prayer. Your rest becomes intercession. Life stops being divided into "spiritual" and "ordinary," because everything becomes sacred when lived in awareness of His presence.

This is the invitation: to turn habits into holy ground. Not striving, but abiding. Not routine, but rhythm. Not religion, but relationship. Because communion is not about visiting God; it's about living with Him. And the more you walk in that rhythm, the more your life will sound like heaven.

The Oil of Intimacy: Fuel for Revival

Every rhythm of communion—every whispered prayer, every pause to listen, every act of adoration—produces oil. Not cheap oil, the kind that burns quick and vanishes, but the costly oil of intimacy pressed in secret. It's the oil that fuels your lamp in the midnight hour, the oil that cannot be borrowed, sold, or faked.

Jesus warned us about this oil. In Matthew 25, ten virgins waited for the Bridegroom. All had lamps, all had been invited—but only five carried oil. The others, distracted and unprepared, discovered too late that passion without intimacy will not last. Their lamps went out at the sound of the midnight cry. That story is not ancient history—it's prophecy. It is speaking now, to us. We are living in the midnight watch, the hour before dawn. The cry has already begun to echo through the earth: *"Behold, the Bridegroom is coming!"* The question is not whether the King will return, but whether the Bride will burn.

The oil of intimacy is not gathered in crowds; it is pressed in closets. It is formed in the stillness of devotion, in the quiet hours when no one applauds, when you turn from the world's scroll to listen for His whisper. Every "yes" you give to His presence becomes a drop of oil. Every fast, every moment of surrender, every song sung through tears fills your vessel a little more.

That oil is preparation. It's what separates the ready from the restless, the enduring from the exhausted. In a world burning out on noise and performance, the ones who have learned to abide in His love will carry fire that does not fade. Their intimacy becomes the lampstand upon which revival rests.

This is why communion cannot remain a concept—it must become a lifestyle. Without oil, the Bride flickers. Without oil, leaders crumble. Without oil, passion turns to performance. But with oil—oh, with oil—the light never goes out. When persecution rises, when darkness deepens, when deception spreads, the burning ones will shine brighter still. Their secret history with God will sustain them when public platforms fall silent.

This is what the oil of intimacy looks like when it is formed in hidden places. When worship lingers long enough to soften hearts. When distraction is laid down in pursuit of His presence. When quiet, faithful prayer rises unseen yet releases fragrance far beyond the walls that contain it. These moments rarely make headlines, but they fuel heaven's purposes on the earth. This is oil. This is revival's fuel.

The coming harvest will not be powered by programs, nor by polished strategies, but by presence. It will not be carried by exhausted orphans running on performance, but by sons and daughters resting in the Father's love. Their intimacy will be their authority. Their secret place will be their strength. And their oil will light the path for multitudes to come home.

So hear the invitation: fill your lamp now. Don't wait for the cry at midnight to go searching. Don't trade your oil for the world's distractions. Don't let your vessel run dry in the hour when light is needed most.

Every moment of communion is a deposit in eternity. Every act of love, every posture of surrender, every choice to abide is oil stored in heaven's reservoir. And when the cry comes—and it will come—you will not panic; you will burn.

This is the Father's strategy for revival: not louder, but deeper. Not faster, but fuller. Not striving, but abiding. He is preparing a Bride whose lamps are trimmed, whose jars overflow, whose love has not grown cold.

The King is coming. The cry is near. And the oil of intimacy—the flame of communion—is the only fire that will last.

My Story: Finding His Voice in the Noise

I have not learned about communion from theory. I have learned it in the noise.

There were seasons when life felt like static—demands pulling at every direction, deadlines shouting louder than peace, headlines feeding fear until silence itself felt impossible. I woke up to the glow of screens, reaching for messages before I reached for mercy. And though I still loved God, the noise kept finding the first word. My spirit felt buried beneath the weight of the urgent.

One morning, weary from the cycle, I reached a breaking point. I set the phone aside, face down on the table, and opened to Psalm 46:10: *"Be still, and know that I am God."* I whispered it aloud, again and again, until my breathing slowed. The verse wasn't just instruction—it was invitation. Stillness began to clear the fog. And in that quiet, His whisper came. Not dramatic. Not loud. Just steady, unmistakable: *"I am here. I have never left."*

That moment marked me. It wasn't a supernatural spectacle—it was a homecoming. I realized I had been chasing what I already had. His voice had not been absent; I had simply been too occupied to hear it.

Since then, I've learned that communion doesn't begin in perfect quiet; it begins in surrendered attention. It starts in the moment you turn down the world and turn your heart toward Him. Sometimes that's five minutes before sunrise. Sometimes it's a whisper on the drive to work. Sometimes it's simply a breath—a pause in the middle of chaos to remember who He is.

Each small choice to give Him the first word builds oil in the lamp. Each pause becomes an altar where the noise bows and peace returns. I've seen it not only in my own life, but in many around me.

These patterns often emerge in ordinary lives when space is made for God's presence. Worship whispered in the midst of responsibility becomes refuge rather than performance. Scripture welcomed at the start of the day begins to order thoughts, decisions, and priorities. Silence chosen over constant input creates room for prayer, and clarity returns where anxiety once lingered.

This is not about exceptional people; it is about ordinary believers choosing extraordinary focus. When room is made for His voice, His presence meets them there. And in that meeting, homes steady, minds clear, and hearts realign with heaven's rhythm.

That is how communion begins—not in grand gestures, but in quiet defiance. Every time you choose His whisper over the world's noise, you make room for the river to flow again.

And here's the wonder: once you begin to hear Him in the stillness, you start to recognize Him everywhere. His presence in the sunrise. His tone in the Scripture. His rhythm in the conversation you almost rushed through. Communion becomes not an event you attend, but a current you live in.

When I think back on those noisy days, I see now that His voice was never gone—it was waiting to be uncovered. The noise was the veil. Stillness was the key.

So if your world feels crowded, if your heart feels heavy, start there.

Turn the phone face down. Open the Word. Breathe His name.

He is not far away. He is waiting at the river's edge, whispering the same invitation He gave the prophets, the shepherds, and the saints:

"Be still, and know that I am God."

In that knowing, everything changes. That is where the noise ends—and communion begins.

The Prophetic Call to Abide

There is a word reverberating in the Spirit right now—clear, insistent, unshakable: Abide.

Not visit. Not sample. Not fit Me in when you can. Abide.

It is the word of survival for the hour we are living in.

The Spirit of God is calling His people out of distraction and into devotion. Out of the noise of temporary pursuits and into the eternal flow of communion. The warfare has intensified because the time is short, and the enemy knows that a distracted Bride is a powerless Bride. He doesn't have to make you sin if he can make you scroll. He doesn't need to tempt you with rebellion if he can seduce you with busyness. If he can steal your stillness, he can weaken your witness.

That is why this word—Abide—carries such holy weight. It is not a gentle suggestion; it is a lifeline. It is heaven's strategy for a Church being shaken.

Jesus said, *"Whoever abides in Me and I in him, he it is that bears much fruit, for apart from Me you can do nothing"* (John 15:5). These are not poetic words; they are prophetic instruction. Apart from Him, ministries crumble. Apart from Him, families fracture. Apart from Him, even good works wither. But in Him—in the river of communion—fruit grows that lasts into eternity.

Abiding is not measured in hours logged or words spoken; it's measured in awareness. It's the posture of the heart that says, *"I will not move without You."* It is the daily reorientation that pulls you out of self-reliance and back into Spirit-dependence. Every time you pause to listen before reacting, you are abiding. Every time you choose peace over panic, presence over pressure, worship over worry—you are abiding.

And in this hour, abiding is warfare. To remain in Christ when the world spins faster every day is to declare rebellion against the systems of Babylon. It's to proclaim with your life, *"I do not belong to the rush of this age. I belong to the rhythm of heaven."*

There is an urgency in this call because the midnight cry is drawing near. The shaking of nations, the rise of deception, the erosion of truth—these are not signs of defeat; they are signals that the Bridegroom is near. And the Bride who abides will not fear.

Abiding will be the difference between those who faint and those who stand. The noise will grow louder, the pressure heavier, the fire hotter. But those who have learned to dwell— who have turned stillness into sanctuary and communion into breath—will endure. Their oil will not run out. Their flame will not flicker. They will carry peace into panic, hope into famine, and light into the darkest hour of history.

This is why abiding must become more than a theme—it must become your rhythm. Abide when the day is busy. Abide when the heart is breaking. Abide when the headlines shake the earth. The secret place you cultivate today will be the shelter that sustains you tomorrow.

I feel this as both warning and promise: the age of borrowed fire is ending. You cannot live off someone else's oil, someone else's revelation, someone else's intimacy. The Bride must carry her own flame. The call is personal. The cry is now.

Hear Him whisper even now through the swirl of the times: *"Abide in Me, and I in you… for apart from Me you can do nothing."*

It's not condemnation—it's compassion. The Father knows the fatigue of His children. He's not demanding more effort; He's offering greater rest. The branch doesn't strive to stay connected—it simply remains. And in remaining, it receives everything.

So pause and feel the gravity of this moment. The Spirit is summoning you—not to more noise, but to deeper nearness. Not to greater performance, but to unbroken presence. Not to hurried service, but to holy stillness. Abide now, and you'll be ready when the trumpet sounds. Abide now, and your lamp will be full when the night grows darkest. Abide now, and your life will bear fruit that will outlast the shaking.

This is not just an invitation—it's a commissioning.

The King is coming, and He's calling His Bride to abide.

A Vision for a Communing Generation

I see it rising—a generation unlike any before it. Not defined by noise, but by nearness. Not marked by platform, but by presence. Not driven by striving, but by surrender.

They move through the earth like quiet rivers—carrying peace into chaos, light into darkness, heaven into ordinary days. Their rhythm is not the pulse of culture but the heartbeat of the Bridegroom. They walk as one, hearts synchronized with heaven, lamps burning with oil pressed in the secret place.

This is the communing generation. Their strength is not in their influence but in their intimacy. Their courage is not in their volume but in their abiding. They do not chase revival meetings—they carry revival within them. Their cry is not for relevance but for radiance. Their goal is not visibility but habitation.

Imagine it with me.

Classrooms becoming prayer rooms as students whisper His name between lessons. Offices turning into sanctuaries as workers pause to listen for His voice before decisions. Kitchens echoing with worship as families break bread and bless the Lord together. Cities quietly pulsing with intercession—hidden voices, unseen hearts—until the atmosphere itself shifts.

This generation lives as if heaven is already here, because in their hearts, it is. They are the fulfillment of Jesus' prayer in John 17: *"That they may all be one, just as You, Father, are in Me, and I in You."* Their unity is not institutional—it's spiritual. It's the oneness that flows from shared intimacy with the same

Spirit. They don't compete for recognition; they complete one another in love. Their connection is communion, not comparison.

These sons and daughters are dismantling Babylon's system without shouting at it. Their rest is their rebellion. Their stillness is their warfare. Their peace disarms principalities. They don't march for attention—they abide for transformation. When they walk into rooms, anxiety begins to lift. When they speak, hope rises. When they pray, cities tremble—not from noise, but from nearness.

I see young men and women lingering at His feet while peers chase applause. I see fathers and mothers building altars of prayer in their homes, turning tables into places of encounter. I see pastors laying down performance and rediscovering the pleasure of His presence. I see elders and grandparents, like Simeon *(Luke 2:29–30)* and Anna *(Luke 2:36–38)*, **called to rest** in intercession and to carry the weight of nations through prayer. Their lamps are trimmed. Their oil is full. Their hearts are unshaken.

And as the world grows darker, they only shine brighter.

This is the Bride the Spirit is preparing—a people who walk with the Wind and burn with holy fire. They have learned the secret of daily communion, and that secret has become their strength. They will carry the gospel not only with words, but with presence. Their very lives will be invitations to encounter the King.

When the world collapses under the weight of anxiety, they will stand in unshakable peace.

When nations rage and systems fail, they will carry the fragrance of the Kingdom. When the midnight cry pierces the sky, they will rise—not scrambling for oil, but blazing with love, ready to meet their Bridegroom.

This is the communing generation—the Esther bride refined by courage, the Joseph company sustained by endurance, the sons and daughters of rest who walk above the sun. Their intimacy is their authority. Their communion is their crown.

And through them, the billion-soul harvest will not be a campaign—it will be a consequence. The world will be drawn not to their brilliance, but to their burning. For the light of His presence resting upon them will illuminate nations, and the knowledge of the glory of the Lord will cover the earth as the waters cover the sea.

The King is coming.

And when He does, He will find a Bride prepared— not exhausted from striving, but radiant from abiding.

For Today: A Prophetic Invitation to Abide

The vision has been spoken, the river revealed, the call released. Now comes the question that only you can answer: Will you step in?

This isn't an invitation for tomorrow. It's for now. The river is flowing today—quiet, constant, holy—and it's waiting for your yes. You were never meant to survive on second-hand oil or yesterday's flame. The world is pulling hard, but the

Spirit is nearer still, whispering, *"Come away. Abide in Me."* This is not a command of burden but of belonging. It is the gentle yet unrelenting call of love—beckoning you out of distraction and into divine rhythm.

You don't have to strive for this presence. You simply have to stay. Abiding is not about doing more; it's about surrendering more. It's resting in the truth that His nearness is your necessity, not your reward.

So today, choose to step back from the noise and return to the river. Choose Scripture before screens. Choose prayer before pressure. Choose stillness before striving. Choose presence over performance. Let your home become His dwelling. Let your heart become His altar. Let your breath become His worship. Because every moment you choose Him first, oil fills your lamp. Every small yes becomes preparation for the great cry that is coming: *"Behold, the Bridegroom is here!"*

This is not about adding another duty—it's about awakening to your design. You were made to walk with God. You were made to carry His presence. You were made to burn with His love.

So here is the invitation, tender yet urgent:

Abide. Abide when you feel His nearness, and abide when you don't. Abide in the light, and abide in the dark. Abide until His whisper becomes the soundtrack of your days and the anchor of your nights.

And as you do, your lamp will stay lit, your oil will stay full, and your heart will stay ready for the hour to come.

This is how revival begins—one abiding heart at a time.

Prayer of Abiding

Jesus, I come to You now.

I lay down the noise, the striving, and the endless rush of the world.

I turn my attention toward Your voice.

Speak, and I will listen.

Whisper, and I will follow.

Let Your river wash through every dry place in me.

Fill my lamp with fresh oil—oil of intimacy, oil of communion, oil that will burn until You return.

Let my life become a sanctuary of Your presence, a resting place for Your Spirit, a living invitation for others to come and see.

Teach me to abide, not visit. Teach me to listen, not rush. Teach me to remain when the world demands motion.

I choose You—today, tomorrow, and forever. You are my source, my strength, my song.

I am Yours.

Abiding, resting, burning—until the day I see You face to face.

Amen.

Beloved, this is your moment.

The same Spirit that walked with Enoch, that sat with Mary, that filled the upper room, is hovering over your life even now.

He is not asking you to earn His nearness—He's inviting you to enjoy it.

The river is flowing.

Step in.

Stay in.

And let your life become the sound of heaven's abiding.

Chapter 10 — Rewriting the Scroll

Introduction — The Mountain Peak

Abiding always leads somewhere.

Stillness is never stagnation—it is preparation. When you linger long enough in the presence of God, the wind begins to shift. The same Spirit who invited you to abide now whispers another invitation: rise. For intimacy is not the end of the journey; it is the birthplace of transformation.

From the quiet river of communion, you begin to sense ascent. The air thins, the noise of the valley fades, and the horizon widens. The Spirit beckons you upward—to the place where revelation meets responsibility, where rest gives birth to purpose. You have dwelt by the waters; now you climb toward the mountain of destiny.

This is the rhythm of the Kingdom: intimacy, then insight; rest, then revelation. What begins at His feet always leads to the mountain where He unveils your scroll. The one who abides learns to ascend—not to escape the world, but to see it from heaven's vantage. Up here, perspective clears. The storms that once surrounded you now swirl beneath your feet. You breathe the air of eternity.

Come with me to the mountain peak. The climb has been long—through the valleys of Joseph's endurance, the battlefield of Esther's courage, the embrace of the Father's love, and the steady river of daily communion. Now, here we stand at the summit. The air is thinner, sharper, filled with a weight that presses on your spirit and clears your vision at the same time. Below, the world churns with noise and chaos—headlines screaming, cultures colliding, lives unraveling. But up here, the noise fades, and the horizon stretches wide, eternal.

This is where God unrolls the scroll. Not the scroll of headlines, not the script the world has written for you, but the scroll penned in eternity—the one He dreamed before you ever drew breath. Psalm 139:16 declares, *"In Your book were written, every one of them, the days that were formed for me, when as yet there were none of them."* Can you see it? A parchment glowing with His fingerprints, etched with fire, carrying the story He authored for you before time began.

So much of life under the sun tries to convince you that your story is already written by circumstance—by betrayal, injustice, delay, or even by the noise of your past. But here, on the mountain peak, Holy Spirit whispers: *"Your scroll is not finished. You are not bound by what was. You are invited into what will be. Trade the world's script for Mine."*

This is not about chasing personal dreams or curating a legacy you control. It is about surrendering to the Author of Life, allowing Him to align every chapter—your victories, your failures, your waiting seasons—with His eternal story. It is about becoming a living letter of His glory in a world desperate for truth.

Think of Joseph. The pit, the prison, the palace—none of them were wasted. Each was a line in his scroll, forged by God's presence, written for a generation starving in famine. Think of Esther. Hidden, crowned, trembling before the king—her scroll unfolded not for her comfort, but for the salvation of her people. And think of your own life. What if every heartbreak, every hidden prayer, every costly yes is ink in the hand of the Author, preparing a story greater than you can see?

We are here now, at the mountain peak, because it is time. Time to take hold of your scroll, to see it not as something fixed and fragile, but as something living and being rewritten in the fire of God's presence. Time to surrender to the pen of the Author who knows the end from the beginning. Time to step into the eternal purpose that will carry you through the shaking and into the harvest.

This is not a moment—it is a movement. Heaven's ink is wet. The parchment is unrolling. The Spirit is summoning you higher.

The only question is: will you let Him rewrite your scroll?

The Scroll of Heaven: Your God-Given Destiny

From the mountain peak, the horizon shifts—and suddenly, you see it.

A scroll, vast and luminous, stretching out from eternity. It is not silent. Its words breathe. Its lines shimmer with life, each one pulsing with the heartbeat of God. This is the scroll of Heaven—your scroll—written by the Author who formed you before your first breath and who still holds the pen.

Jeremiah heard it first as a whisper: *"Before I formed you in the womb I knew you, and before you were born I consecrated you"* (Jeremiah 1:5).

David sang it as revelation: *"In Your book were written, every one of them, the days that were formed for me, when as yet there were none of them"* (Psalm 139:16).

And John, exiled on Patmos, saw it in glory—a scroll sealed in the right hand of the One who sits upon the throne (Revelation 5).

Every prophet, every psalmist, every seer caught the same glimpse: your life was written before time began, authored in love, secured in eternity.

But here lies the mystery—scrolls can be tampered with.

The enemy has always sought to smear ink across the parchment of destiny, to convince sons and daughters that their story is too stained, too shattered, too far gone to be redeemed. Babylon's counterfeit scripts shimmer with false light: success without surrender, influence without intimacy, pleasure without purpose. They promise much and deliver nothing. They feed the soul but starve the spirit.

Many live and die by these false scrolls—edited by fear, rewritten by culture, defined by pain. But Heaven's scroll is untouchable. It cannot be erased; it can only be reclaimed. It waits for your yes.

Rewriting your scroll does not mean erasing your past—it means redeeming it.

The ink of Heaven doesn't cover in shame; it transforms in glory. Every line the enemy meant for destruction becomes the place where God writes redemption. Every scar becomes a sentence of salvation. Every wound becomes a word of testimony. This is not denial of what has been—it is divine reclamation of what was lost.

Joseph understood this. His scroll carried betrayal, false accusation, and years of silence. Yet at its end, he declared, *"You meant evil against me, but God meant it for good"* (Genesis 50:20). His story bore scars—but they glowed with glory. What the enemy wrote as ruin became the ink of restoration for nations.

Your scroll is no different. Heaven wastes nothing. The pages the world discards are often the very ones God highlights. What once brought you shame will become the line that shakes kingdoms.

So here, on the mountain peak, the question stands before you like fire:

Which scroll will you live from?

The brittle pages of the world's script—or the living scroll of Heaven?

One chains you to what was. The other calls you into what will be.

One leaves you exhausted, chasing relevance. The other anchors you in eternal purpose.

One fades with time. The other endures forever.

The Spirit is calling: *"Lay down the false script. Take up the scroll that carries My breath. Let Me write My glory into your days."*

The pen is in His hand—but the surrender is in yours.

Will you place your story back into the Author's keeping? Will you trust Him to write through the ashes, through the waiting, through the questions you can't yet answer?

Lift your eyes again from the mountain.

Can you see it now?

Your scroll—glowing, living, breathing—unrolling before you like dawn breaking over the horizon. The ink is alive. The Author is near. The invitation is now.

It is time to reclaim what was written before the world ever spoke your name.

It is time to let Heaven write again.

Jeremiah: A Prophet's Scroll Rewritten

If Heaven holds the pen, Jeremiah's life shows what happens when the ink runs through trembling hands.

His story is not one of ease but of endurance—a prophetic mirror for every heart that has ever felt too small for the call.

The word of the Lord came to Jeremiah not in triumph, but in hesitation.

"Before I formed you in the womb I knew you, and before you were born I consecrated you; I appointed you a prophet to the nations" (Jeremiah 1:5).

But Jeremiah protested: *"Ah, Lord God! Behold, I do not know how to speak, for I am only a youth"* (v. 6).

He read his scroll through the lens of limitation, measuring divine calling by human adequacy. But the Author interrupted the narrative:

"Do not say, 'I am only a youth'; for to all to whom I send you, you shall go, and whatever I command you, you shall speak" (v. 7).

In that moment, Heaven began rewriting his scroll—not with flattery, but with fire.

Jeremiah's assignment was costly. He carried words that burned but were rarely welcomed.

He was mocked, beaten, imprisoned, misunderstood. There were days he wanted to quit, to silence the message, to throw the scroll into the flames. *"I will not mention Him, or speak any more in His name,"* he confessed (Jeremiah 20:9). But the fire would not let him go. *"His word is in my heart like a fire, a fire shut up in my bones; I am weary of holding it in; indeed, I cannot."*

Even when the king himself took Jeremiah's written scroll and cut it to pieces—feeding it line by line into the fire (Jeremiah 36:23)—the Author refused to lose the story.

The Lord simply said, *"Take another scroll and write on it all the former words that were in the first scroll… and also many similar words were added to them"* (Jeremiah 36:28, 32).

What man tried to destroy, God expanded. Every word burned in the fire came back multiplied. Every line meant to be silenced became a louder witness of Heaven's perseverance. That is the power of divine authorship—no fire, no rejection, no opposition can erase what God has decreed.

When you belong to the Author, even what feels lost in the flames becomes fresh ink in His hand.

Jeremiah learned that his scroll was not about personal success or human validation. It was about obedience—about letting the Word of the Lord move through him, even when it broke him.

Perhaps you recognize that same tension. You've carried words that seemed too heavy for your voice. You've faced rejection for truth spoken in love. You've felt silenced by fear or exhaustion. Maybe you've even tried to bury your calling, convinced it's safer to stay quiet. But the fire will not die—it was never yours to extinguish.

The scroll of your life is still in motion. What others tried to cut out, God is rewriting with greater authority.

This pattern repeats itself wherever God is allowed to work deeply. What the world dismisses as weakness becomes a vessel for prophetic clarity. What shame once tried to bury becomes oil for healing. Compassion carries authority that intellect alone never could, and scars—when surrendered— become places where grace flows freely.

These lives echo Jeremiah's truth: God does not need unblemished parchment to write His glory. He writes on surrendered hearts, and His words endure far beyond the moment. What once looked like disqualification becomes the very testimony through which His faithfulness is revealed.

Jeremiah's life stands as a monument to every weary messenger, every heart afraid its words have fallen flat. The Author does not lose His drafts. What He begins, He completes. The scroll may burn, but the message remains. The fire that once felt destructive will become the very flame that defines you.

So if you find yourself standing in ashes, don't despair. Look again—the Author is still writing. The pen is steady. The ink is eternal. The story is not over.

Every tear you've shed has become ink. Every rejection has become space for revelation. Every "too late" has become a margin where God writes, "I am not finished."

This is the beauty of a rewritten scroll: the fire that once threatened to erase you becomes the proof that you were chosen to carry flame.

Paul: From Persecutor to Apostle

If Jeremiah's scroll revealed divine appointment through anguish, Paul's reveals redemption through encounter.

His story is not one of slow awakening—it is an explosion of light. One moment, the hunter of believers. The next, blinded by the glory he had long resisted.

On the road to Damascus, the Author's pen paused mid-sentence and rewrote the entire narrative. Heaven broke into time. The scroll of a man once bound by law was pierced by grace, and inked anew by the hand of the Redeemer Himself.

"Saul, Saul, why are you persecuting Me?"

The voice thundered, but it was not condemnation—it was invitation. In one breath, the Living Word dismantled his false zeal and revealed the face of mercy.

When his eyes opened again, the world was no longer divided into categories of holy and unholy, worthy and unworthy. It was all Christ. All grace. All new creation.

That is the power of divine authorship—

to take a life written in opposition to truth and transform it into the very vessel that carries truth to the ends of the earth.

In Paul's story, we see the mystery of God's pen: redemption is not an edit; it is a resurrection.

Heaven did not discard Saul's intellect, passion, or discipline. It redeemed them. The same fervor that once fueled persecution became the fire of apostleship. The same sharpness that once cut down others now carved letters of revelation across continents. What was once zeal without knowledge became wisdom burning with Spirit.

When Paul later wrote, *"I press on to take hold of that for which Christ Jesus took hold of me,"* he was not speaking as a man still chasing redemption—he was writing as one overtaken by it.

Every line of his scroll pulsed with the awareness that he no longer belonged to his own narrative. He was possessed by a greater story.

The Author had not just changed his direction; He had claimed his identity.

So it is with us.

The scrolls of our lives are not destroyed when grace enters; they are rewritten with divine continuity. Every detour becomes a doorway. Every failure, a footnote of mercy.

God wastes nothing—not even our rebellion. The same ink that once recorded sin becomes the medium through which grace testifies.

Paul's conversion is not an ancient tale—it is a mirror. Every encounter with the risen Christ demands a rewriting. Every blinding light calls for surrendered sight. And every heart once hardened by pride is invited to become parchment soft enough for the Spirit's ink.

When Heaven holds the pen, even the persecutor becomes a preacher. Even the accuser becomes the advocate. Even the enemy of grace becomes its greatest herald. This is the transformation of the scroll—when human will bows, and divine authorship begins to write.

And so, the question arises once more: Will you allow the Author to take your pen? To turn your Damascus road into a doorway of destiny? To make the very chapter that once shamed you the one that sets others free? Look again at Paul's story.

It is not about a man who found God—it is about God who found a man and refused to let him live beneath his calling. That same love still writes. That same ink still flows. That same Author still redeems the unfinished manuscripts of our lives—one encounter at a time.

John: The Beloved and the Revelation of Love

If Jeremiah shows us calling through fire, and Paul shows us redemption through encounter, then John reveals the final ascent — transformation through intimacy.

His scroll was not forged in resistance or rebellion, but in relationship. He didn't wrestle like Jeremiah or collide like Paul; he leaned.

Among the Twelve, John was the one who dared to draw near.

While others debated who was greatest, John rested against the chest of Jesus — listening not for information, but for heartbeat. He found what striving could never earn: proximity. And from that posture, revelation flowed.

This is the secret of divine authorship: the deeper the intimacy, the clearer the ink.

John's writings carry a different fragrance — not the dust of the road, but the scent of the throne room.

His gospel begins not with Bethlehem, but with eternity.

"In the beginning was the Word, and the Word was with God, and the Word was God."

He had heard the heartbeat of the Eternal Word, and his own language became flame. Love was his lens. When others saw miracles, John saw affection. When others fled the cross, John stayed. He stood beside the broken body of the One he loved, and in that grief, his scroll was sealed with revelation: that love is not sentiment — it is sacrifice. That true power is not dominion — it is devotion.

And so, when exile came — the silence of Patmos, the sting of isolation — love did not fade; it expanded. What began as a whisper on Jesus' chest became thunder in heaven. The man who once leaned now beheld the Lamb. The one who knew His heartbeat now saw His glory unveiled. And the Spirit said, *"Write what you see."*

The beloved became the scribe of eternity. This is the progression of the mountain. Jeremiah teaches obedience in pain. Paul reveals grace in redemption. But John unveils the summit — the revelation of love that transforms obedience into union and redemption into worship.

For on the heights of intimacy, revelation is no longer something you receive — it is someone you become.

John's name means *"Yahweh is gracious."* And that grace was his message. He began his story at the table, and ended it in the throne room. He began with the touch of a hand, and ended with the vision of a King. He began as a son of thunder and became the apostle of love.

That is what happens when you let love rewrite your scroll — noise turns to knowing, striving turns to seeing, and zeal turns to rest.

Perhaps that's the invitation for us now. Not merely to write about God, but to lean until His heartbeat becomes our rhythm. Not merely to work for Him, but to abide until His Word burns through our being. Not merely to prophesy, but to become prophecy — a living scroll of love, written by the very hand of the One we adore. Because in the end, John's revelation is not a map of end-times — it is a portrait of intimacy. It is the unveiling of a Bride who mirrors her Bridegroom. It is the crescendo of the divine romance — the story of a God who not only calls and redeems, but rests within His beloved until love itself becomes the testimony of the age.

The War for Your Scroll in These Days

Love always births war. Because whatever Heaven writes, hell tries to erase. The more clearly you carry His likeness, the more fiercely the counterfeit fights for your attention.

This is the hour of the scroll wars — the battle for authorship over human identity, destiny, and devotion.

From Eden's whisper to Babylon's roar, the enemy has always targeted the written word of God.

"Did God really say?" — it was the first lie, and it still echoes.

He could not steal the throne, so he sought to distort the script. He cannot create, so he counterfeits.

And in this generation, his weapons are subtler but sharper — distraction, distortion, and digital domination.

The war for your scroll is not fought in paper and ink, but in attention and agreement. Every voice that competes for your focus is vying for authorship. Every algorithm that shapes your desires is trying to co-write your story.

The question is no longer simply Who are you? — but Whose narrative are you living?

Culture now prints its own gospels.

- "You are your platform."
- "You are your past."
- "You are your performance."
- "You are your pain."

They are the four false evangelists of Babylon, preaching identity apart from intimacy. But the scroll of Heaven still declares: *"You are Mine."* Not because of output, but because of origin. Not because of fame, but because of Fatherhood.

John's revelation showed us what happens when intimacy wins — a scroll sealed in Heaven's hand, unbreakable except by the Lamb.

But our age has forged counter-scrolls: narratives that enslave sons and daughters to approval, consumption, and fear.

Cancel culture is more than a trend; it is a tactic.

It teaches shame as justice and silence as safety, punishing repentance and glorifying rebellion.

It aims to make you believe your story is over, that your chapter cannot be redeemed. But Heaven says otherwise. The

Lion of Judah still breaks seals. The Author still writes through ashes. The ink of mercy still flows for those who will return to the mountain and say, *"Lord, write again."*

This is why discernment has never been more vital. When the scroll of truth and the scroll of deception unroll side by side, only intimacy will tell them apart. The voice that leaned on Jesus will recognize His tone even when the world twists His words. The Bride who abides will not fall for Babylon's brilliance. Her lamp is full, her scroll sealed by fire, her gaze fixed on the Author's eyes.

Look around — the war is visible everywhere. Children scrolling themselves numb, losing wonder before they find purpose. Leaders burning out under the pressure to perform instead of abiding in presence. Nations rewriting morality as though Heaven has gone silent. But God is not mute. His scrolls are still being opened. His sons and daughters are still being commissioned. His ink is still wet on willing hearts.

You were born for this hour — not to echo the world's noise, but to guard Heaven's narrative. To stand as a living scroll, uncorrupted, unedited, unmarred by compromise. To carry words that burn, not because you crafted them, but because the Author inscribed them through your surrender. This is the war for your scroll.

It is not a battle for relevance, but for revelation. Not a fight for influence, but for integrity. The enemy wants your agreement; Heaven wants your allegiance. The choice is made daily: which script will you amplify — Babylon's lie or Heaven's line? The Spirit is sounding the alarm. The time for passive faith is over. This is the hour of holy writers — men and women who live so close to His voice that their lives become ink. Every prayer, every fast, every whispered "yes" becomes a strike against darkness. Every surrender of the pen becomes rebellion against Babylon's counterfeit authorship.

Guard your scroll. Feed your lamp. Abide in His love. Because the war for your story is the war for this generation's harvest. And when the midnight cry comes, it will not be the loud who are heard — it will be the ones who never stopped listening.

Rewriting Your Scroll: A Daily Surrender

Every battle must lead to surrender. Not the surrender of defeat, but the surrender of authorship. For the war for your scroll is not won by striving harder—it is won by yielding deeper. Heaven's victory is never forced; it is written through consent. Every day, the Author waits for one simple offering: your "yes." Rewriting your scroll is not about erasing what was written—it's about redeeming what remains. It's about handing back the pen you've gripped too tightly, trusting that His handwriting can turn even the jagged lines of your past into a masterpiece of grace.

The psalmist captured it best: *"Your word is a lamp to my feet and a light to my path."* (Psalm 119:105)

Notice—it's not a floodlight for your lifetime, but a lamp for your next step. The Author doesn't rush the story; He writes in rhythm with your obedience. One step of surrender at a time. The world tells you to take control—to build your own brand, direct your own plot, protect your own image.

But control is the enemy of creativity, and fear is the thief of revelation. When you try to write your own scroll, you limit it to human ink. But when you surrender the pen, divine ink begins to flow—ink that heals, redeems, and multiplies far beyond your reach.

This is the mystery of partnership with Heaven: God does not need your perfection; He needs your permission. He will not coerce the script of your life—He will co-author it through your surrender. Each morning, He waits for you to whisper, "Write through me today." And when you do, the line between your voice and His begins to blur.

Your decisions carry His tone.

Your work bears His breath.

Your life becomes the Word made visible in your generation.

Rewriting your scroll is not a one-time altar moment; it's a rhythm.

It's the sacred exchange that happens when you open your Bible before your phone, when you pause to listen before you react, when you pray before you plan, when you forgive before you justify.

Each act of obedience is another word written in heaven's ink.

Each "yes" becomes light to the next line.

It might look small—quiet choices in the secret place, gentle corrections of heart and thought—but this is where revival begins.

The most powerful stories are not written in headlines but in hidden rooms, where surrendered hearts say again and again: *"Not my will, but Yours."*

Paul called it walking in the Spirit. (Galatians 5:25) It is not a sprint—it's a rhythm. The Spirit whispers the next word, and you walk it out. He corrects the punctuation, and you yield. He edits with mercy, and you rest in trust. The story unfolds not by force, but by flow. And here's the beauty: the Author never wastes ink. Even your detours become dialogue in His redemptive story. Even your delays become white space where His grace breathes. Even your heartbreak becomes poetry that ministers to others when the ink dries.

He is not rewriting to erase you—He is rewriting to reveal Himself through you. This truth unfolds again and again wherever hearts are surrendered to God's authorship. What is lost is not simply restored—it is rewritten. Purpose is no longer found in rebuilding what once was, but in allowing God to write something new, line by line, prayer by prayer. Pain, when yielded, does not disappear; it is transformed. What once wounded becomes wisdom. What once felt wasted becomes weighty with meaning.

This is what surrender does. It does not merely redeem pain— it multiplies it into purpose. That is the nature of divine authorship.

So what does it look like for you?

Maybe it's as simple as whispering, "Lord, what are You writing today?" before you begin your work. Maybe it's renouncing the false authors—the fear, pride, shame, or comparison—that have tried to seize your pen. Maybe it's trusting that the same hand that wrote your beginning already knows your ending. Rewriting your scroll is not about perfection; it's about permission. Let Him write again. Because the greatest revival will not begin in pulpits—it will begin in rewritten lives.

Each surrendered scroll becomes a spark. Each yes becomes oil. Each testimony becomes a torch that lights the way for another soul out of Babylon's narrative and back into Heaven's design.

So pause here, on this mountain of surrender.

Lift your pen.

Lay it down.

And listen as Heaven whispers over you once more: *"My child, your story is not over. My ink has not dried. Hand Me your scroll, and watch what I will write."*

The Oil of Destiny: Fuel for Revival

Every act of surrender produces oil.

Every hidden yes becomes fuel.

Every tear that falls on the altar becomes a drop of anointing for the days ahead. This is the mystery of destiny — it is not powered by ambition, but by oil pressed in surrender.

When Jesus spoke of the ten virgins in Matthew 25, He was not describing spiritual hierarchy — He was describing spiritual readiness.

All ten had lamps.

All ten carried purpose.

But only five carried oil.

When the midnight cry came — *"Behold, the Bridegroom is coming!"* — the difference was not desire, but devotion.

Not gifting, but intimacy. Not activity, but alignment. Oil is costly because it cannot be borrowed. You cannot inherit another's surrender. You cannot purchase another's intimacy. Oil is forged in the fire of your own daily "yes." It is the invisible currency of Heaven — pressed from obedience, refined in waiting, poured out in worship. It is what keeps your lamp burning when others fade.

This oil is not for comfort; it is for commission. Each drop that fills your vessel becomes fuel for something far greater than survival — it becomes light for the nations.

Revelation 19:7 declares, *"The marriage of the Lamb has come, and His Bride has made herself ready."*

The Bride's readiness is not measured by performance or perfection — but by oil.

By love that has endured testing. By lamps that have burned through the long night of delay. By hearts that have surrendered the pen and stayed lit in hidden rooms when no one was watching. This is the oil of destiny.

Joseph carried it into Pharaoh's court, and the nations ate during famine. Esther carried it into the throne room, and her people lived through decree. You carry it into this generation — not as theory, but as presence.

Every time you say "yes" when no one applauds, Heaven adds oil to your lamp. Every time you forgive instead of resent, worship instead of worry, surrender instead of strive, your vessel fills.

And when the shaking comes, it will not be the most gifted who stand — it will be the most filled. This oil burns beyond your lifetime.

It is generational.

It runs down like Psalm 133's anointing — from the head to the beard, to the edges of the garment, touching every son and daughter who stands beneath it. Each surrendered life becomes a conduit of inheritance. A father's "yes" becomes oil on his children's heads. A mother's worship becomes covering for her descendants. A generation's obedience becomes fire for the one that follows. This is the multiplication of surrender — the compounding interest of devotion.

These glimpses point to a deeper pattern—the hidden exchange that sustains true revival. When influence is laid down in favor of prayer, authority emerges that does not depend on microphones or platforms. When worship is offered in the midst of suffering, homes become saturated with heaven's presence. When prayer is carried faithfully in obscurity, oil accumulates in ways that only God records.

This is the quiet economy of the Kingdom. What is surrendered in secret becomes strength in the open. What is poured out unseen becomes fuel when the flame is tested.

This is the hidden exchange that sustains revival. Programs may ignite emotion, but only oil sustains flame. Charisma may draw a crowd, but only intimacy births endurance.

The Bride's lamps must burn with more than borrowed fire; they must be soaked in the oil of surrender.

And here's the holy paradox: *Oil is not produced in moments of victory, but in seasons of pressure.*

Like olives in the press, your greatest pain often yields your purest oil. The crushing becomes consecration. The waiting becomes refining. The very thing the enemy meant to extinguish you becomes the reason your flame burns brighter.

This is why your surrender matters. Because your oil is not just for you — it is for the harvest.

It is for the billion souls yet to see the light.

It is for the Bride who must shine through the darkness before the dawn. When you surrender the pen, when you let Him rewrite your scroll, you are not just yielding your life — you are fueling a generation. The war for your scroll is the war for this oil.

The enemy cannot steal your salvation, so he aims for your surrender. He wants your vessel empty, your lamp flickering, your story unwritten.

But every time you kneel, you refill. Every time you worship through weariness, you overflow. Every time you align with the Author's will, you add oil to the lamp of destiny.

Hear this clearly: your "yes" today is not small. It echoes in eternity. Your hidden obedience writes light into the future. Your surrendered scroll becomes a torch that will burn long after your lifetime. And together — your oil, my oil, the Church's oil — will form the flame that announces His return.

This is the oil of destiny: Pressed in private. Poured in love. Burning in unity. Fuel for the final harvest. The King is coming. And when the cry pierces the night, may your lamp be full, your scroll be open, and your life be aflame with the oil of surrender.

My Story: Surrendering to His Pen

There was a season when I believed the ink of my story had dried — when the pages of my life felt fixed, sealed by failure and time.

I looked back and saw smudged lines, unfinished chapters, relationships strained, prayers unanswered.

I thought the pen had slipped from my hand, that my scroll was beyond repair.

But that's where the Author met me. Not at the height of victory, but in the silence between sentences. Not in the noise of performance, but in the stillness where surrender speaks louder than striving. And in that quiet place, Holy Spirit whispered the words that redefined everything: *"Your scroll is still in My hand."* That one sentence became a turning point.

I realized I had spent years trying to write my own redemption — to edit my story through effort, to revise pain through reason, to force restoration through control.

But grace does not edit; it rewrites. Mercy doesn't erase what was; it transforms it into testimony. When I finally laid down my pen, the Author picked it up again. Not to shame me, but to show me that He had never stopped writing.

He began to highlight moments I had dismissed — prayers whispered in weakness, acts of faith no one saw, tears shed in secret. He wove them together, revealing that what I thought were wasted years were actually the spaces where His ink soaked deepest.

The pauses I mistook for abandonment were paragraphs of preparation. And then came the realization that changed me forever: Even the ache can become anointing. Even the longing can become oil. Even the chapters I wish I could rewrite are now part of the divine narrative that brings Him glory. So, I began to live differently. I stopped asking Him to fix the story and started asking Him to finish it. I began to see every day as a blank page, every moment as a chance for His voice to shape the next line.

When I prayed, it wasn't *"Lord, make this go away,"* but *"Lord, make this mean something."* And He did.

New doors opened—not of ambition, but of intercession. Conversations became divine appointments. Prayers once soaked in tears began to carry power. I watched the ink of His redemption dry into words that only He could have written.

The story that once felt fractured became fuel for others walking through their own rewriting.

This same pattern reveals itself wherever God is given permission to work deeply. What once enslaved no longer defines. What once silenced becomes a voice of healing. Lives marked by brokenness are not discarded—they are rewritten, carrying peace, purity, and authority that ripple far beyond themselves.

This is the truth they discover: the scroll does not end in the fire—it is rewritten through it. What passes through the flame is not destroyed, but refined. And what emerges carries weight that can only be forged in surrender.

This is what it means to surrender the pen. It's not losing control—it's gaining alignment. It's discovering that what you feared would disqualify you is the very ink Heaven uses to authenticate your story. It's trusting that the Author knows how to weave redemption through the ruins until glory overshadows grief.

So if you're standing where I once stood—holding a pen that feels heavy with regret or hesitation—hear this: You are not too late. The story is not finished. The Author is still writing. The ink of His mercy never runs dry. And if you'll place your pen in His hand again, you'll see Him take every broken sentence and turn it into a declaration of victory. Because that's what He does. He turns ashes into ink. He turns silence into song. He turns stories into scrolls that outlive their writers. Your surrender is not the end of your story.

It is the beginning of His.

The Prophetic Call to Rewrite

I feel the weight of this as I write— this is not just my story; it is ours.

The Spirit of God is moving across the earth with a pen of fire in His hand, searching for those who will say yes to being rewritten.

He is standing before His people — before you — asking the same question He asked the prophets, the apostles, the saints of old:

"Will you trust Me with your scroll?"

There is a war for authorship in this hour.

The enemy wants to define your narrative — through shame, failure, distraction, and fear — until you forget who wrote your name in the first place.

He wants you to believe that your story is already sealed, that your destiny is bound by your past or limited by circumstance.

But Heaven is releasing a divine interruption — a rewriting movement where lives, families, and even nations are being pulled out of Babylon's script and rewritten into God's redemptive storyline.

This is not poetic language; it is prophecy.

The Author of Life is calling His people to rebellion — not against Him, but against every false pen that has tried to claim their identity.

Rest was rebellion in Chapter 7. Grief refined us in Chapter 8 —teaching us to remain seated with Christ while love and loss are still unresolved on the earth. Communion became warfare in Chapter 9. Now, rewriting your scroll is alignment —the holy exchange where we lay down the narratives written in fear and take up the one written in fire.

It is the moment when you stop reading from the world's manuscript and begin to speak from Heaven's. You can feel this call rising like thunder beneath the surface of history.

A shaking has come upon the earth — political, cultural, spiritual — because God is confronting the counterfeit authors.

Every system built on pride is being exposed.

Every false identity rooted in performance is being stripped away. And in the midst of this shaking, He is awakening His scribes of fire — sons and daughters whose stories will no longer echo Babylon but radiate the handwriting of Heaven.

When Jeremiah thought he was too young, God rewrote his scroll. When Paul thought he was too guilty, God rewrote his scroll. When John thought he was too exiled, God gave him Revelation. And now the same Spirit that hovered over their pages is hovering over yours.

He is ready to write again — to reclaim every chapter the enemy has tried to hijack, to redeem every line that fear has blurred, to inscribe hope where shame once stained the margins.

This call is not for the comfortable. It is for those who are done with self-authorship. It is for those who are weary of scrolling through borrowed identities and ready to burn with the story God has been waiting to tell. It is for a Bride who refuses to be defined by the world's ink and chooses instead to be written by the Lamb.

When you hand Him your scroll, your life ceases to be a collection of disconnected moments — it becomes prophecy.

Every surrendered yes echoes into eternity. Every hidden obedience becomes a line in the great story of redemption. And together, these lives form the manuscript of a generation rising in radiant defiance of darkness. So hear the call clearly: Lay down the false scripts. Break partnership with every narrative that doesn't sound like love. Renounce the ink of fear, shame, and striving. And hand Him your scroll. For the

Spirit of the Lord is saying: *"My children, I am rewriting the stories of this generation. I am redeeming the chapters you thought were lost. I am resurrecting callings buried by disappointment. I am releasing fresh ink upon your lives, your families, your nations. Do not fear the blank page — it is holy ground. For I, the Author, am faithful to finish what I began."*

This is the prophetic call to rewrite — not to dream bigger, but to surrender deeper. Not to build your own name, but to bear His. Not to edit your story, but to let it burn. Because when your life becomes a scroll in His hand, your testimony becomes revival.

Your obedience becomes oil.

Your yes becomes the ink that writes hope into the generations to come. So lift your eyes to the mountain once more. The Author is standing before you, pen in hand. He is not finished. He is just beginning. Heaven's ink is still wet — and your next chapter is waiting to be written.

A Vision for a Scroll-Rewritten Generation

I see it—clear as fire on the horizon, a vision forming in the Spirit.

A generation rising, scrolls in hand, eyes lifted, hearts burning with the ink of Heaven. They are not defined by what they have done but by what has been written about them before time began.

They are the sons and daughters of restoration—rebels against Babylon's narrative, authors of revival, living epistles that the world can no longer ignore.

These are not the polished or the perfect. They are the rewritten. The once-broken, now burning. The formerly lost, now luminous. They carry redemption in their bones and truth in their breath.

They have traded the world's applause for the whisper of the Author's voice. Their scrolls glow with holy fire—each line alive with the fingerprints of grace.

Picture it.

Classrooms transformed into upper rooms, where students gather not to compete but to commune, declaring, "Lord, write Your story through us."

Living rooms turned sanctuaries, where families lay down devices and lift up prayers, speaking identity over children who will never know the orphan spirit.

Offices and boardrooms humming with the presence of God, decisions shaped by heaven's ink instead of ambition's pen.

Churches stripped of pretense and performance, becoming scriptoriums of glory—places where the Spirit dictates fresh chapters of revival.

I see young men and women who no longer chase platforms but presence.

They fast from noise to hear His whisper.

They walk through culture's fire without the smell of smoke, because their lives are already sealed in flame.

Their purity is their protest. Their humility is their authority. Their intimacy is their influence. I see parents rewriting legacies in real time—fathers blessing, mothers prophesying, children responding with songs that shift atmospheres. I see pastors and prophets laying down the pursuit of notoriety and picking up intercession again, preaching from tears instead of trends. I see artists painting visions straight from the throne, writers penning words that breathe life into nations, musicians releasing frequencies that dismantle despair. And I see elders—those who once thought their season had passed— lifting trembling hands and saying, "He is writing again."

Dreams once buried under disappointment resurrect as intercession. Their prayers become the ink that saturates this generation's scrolls. *This is not mere imagination—it is intercession moving toward fulfillment.*

Joel 2 is alive again: *"I will pour out My Spirit on all flesh; your sons and your daughters shall prophesy."* Prophecy is not performance—it is participation. It is Heaven dictating its story through yielded vessels. When sons and daughters prophesy, the scrolls of the earth begin to realign with the books of Heaven.

I see this scroll-rewritten generation walking in divine synchronization. They live above the sun, yet move through the earth with compassion. Their footsteps echo the Lamb's. Their speech carries the cadence of eternity. Their lives are interwoven into the great manuscript of redemption—each sentence amplifying the glory of the Author.

And this movement will not fade. It will multiply. One rewritten scroll ignites another until cities, nations, and generations become libraries of testimony.

The false scripts of Babylon—fear, lust, pride, greed—will burn in the fire of holy surrender, and in their place, the language of Heaven will flood the earth again.

Habakkuk's prophecy will be fulfilled before our eyes: "The earth will be filled with the knowledge of the glory of the Lord as the waters cover the sea."

This is the vision. A global Bride, radiant with intimacy, her lamps full of oil, her scrolls blazing with revelation. She is not timid. She is not tired. She has been rewritten in the ink of love and clothed in the garment of surrender. When the world trembles, she stands. When darkness deepens, she shines.

When the midnight cry resounds, she lifts her scroll high and declares, *"The King is coming!"* And He will recognize His handwriting upon her.

He will see His story written across her life and call her by name. Because this is what it means to be rewritten—to live as a living letter from Heaven, known and read by all, authored by the One who never fails to finish what He begins.

So arise, scroll-rewritten generation. Do not hand your life to the counterfeit pens of culture. Do not settle for the narratives of fear and fame. Lift your parchment toward the flame of His Spirit and let Him write. The ink is wet. The Author is near.

And the story He is writing through you will set the world ablaze.

For Today: A Prophetic Invitation to Rewrite

The scroll is in your hands. Heaven is leaning close. This is not theory. It is not poetry. It is the moment between heartbeats where eternity touches time.

The Author of Life—the One who spoke galaxies into being and wrote your name before the foundation of the world—is asking for the pen.

Today is not about fixing what was; it is about surrendering what is. It is not about rewriting your past through effort, but releasing your future through obedience. This is the sound of divine invitation: *"Will you let Me write again?"*

Every lie that has claimed authorship over your life—shame, fear, striving, regret—bows here.

Every false script that has whispered, *"You've gone too far,"* or *"It's too late,"* burns in the fire of His mercy.

The same hand that wrote *"It is finished"* on the Cross now stretches toward you, offering restoration with every drop of redeemed ink.

Lay it down.
The pen.
The pressure.
The need to control how your story ends.
The Author never asked you to write alone.
He only asked you to yield the parchment.

You've seen how Joseph's endurance, Esther's courage, the Father's embrace, and daily communion have all led here—to this mountain moment, where your scroll meets His flame. Now, all of Heaven waits for your yes.

Because when you surrender the pen, the rewriting begins. When you trust His authorship, alignment unfolds. And when you hand Him your life, revival is born.

This is your rebellion against Babylon's system. This is your roar in the face of the enemy:

"I will not live by your script. My life is not defined by fear, shame, or failure. I belong to the Author of Life, and only His words will define my days."

So pause here—between the old chapter and the new.
Let the silence become holy.
Take a deep breath.
Feel the weight of His love pressing gently against your heart.
You don't have to earn it. You don't have to prove it.
You only have to receive it.
Because every surrender becomes a sentence, and every yes becomes a line in the story Heaven is waiting to tell through you.

Here is your invitation, as real as the ink on this page:

1. Surrender your pen.
Whisper it out loud: *"Lord, I give You my story."*
You cannot lose what you give to God; you only discover what it was always meant to be.

2. Break agreement with false authorship.
Say no to every voice that has tried to edit your worth.
Every lie that says *"you are what you've done"* ends here.

3. Declare your true identity.
Speak it until your heart believes it: *"I am His workmanship, created for good works, prepared before time began."* (Ephesians 2:10)

4. Step into the next chapter.
Ask Him, *"Lord, what do You want to write through me today?"*
Then listen. Move. Obey. Even small steps echo in eternity.

And now, a prayer—a declaration of surrender for those who are ready to live as rewritten scrolls of Heaven:

Prayer of Surrender
Lord, here is my life—my story, my past, my future.
I surrender the pen.
Redeem every word written in pain, and rewrite every line with Your truth.
Burn away the false scripts that have shaped me, and inscribe Your promises deep within my heart.
Let my life become a living letter, read by this world and known by You.
I choose Your authorship over my own.
I choose surrender over striving.
I choose Your glory over my comfort.
Write through me, Lord, until my story becomes the sound of revival.
In Jesus' name—Amen.

This is your moment.
The ink of Heaven is still wet.
The parchment of your life is open.
And the Author stands ready to write.

Do not delay.
Do not doubt.
Lift your scroll toward the flame.

Because what He writes next will not only redeem your past—
it will awaken generations yet to come.

Epilogue — The Ink of Eternity

The mountain is quiet now. The wind has settled into a whisper.

The scroll lies open in your hands—warm from the flame, alive with new words that only Heaven could write.

You are no longer who you were when this ascent began. Something eternal has shifted.

The same Spirit who called you to endure, to rise, to rest, and to abide now marks you with purpose.

You are a rewritten scroll—an echo of His authorship, a vessel of His story, a flame that will not fade.

And as you descend the mountain, carrying His words within you, know this:

what He began in secret will speak in the streets; what He wrote in fire will shine in the dark.

Your life is not closing—it is opening.

The Author is still writing, the ink of eternity still flowing, and the next chapter is already being formed in His heart.

So walk gently, but boldly.

Live as one whose story belongs above the sun.

For Heaven has spoken, and the scroll in your hands is alive.

Conclusion — The Final Call: Live Above the Sun

Come with me to the throne room of heaven, where the air hums with glory, the light of the King shines brighter than a thousand suns, and every heartbeat echoes His eternal purpose. Stand here, at the edge of eternity, and look back over the journey we've walked—through the weight of the world, the battle of the mind, the beholding that transforms, the endurance of Joseph, the fire of Spirit-led living, the courage of Esther, the rest of the Father, the rhythm of communion, and the rewriting of your scroll.

This is not the end of the story. It is the beginning of your call to live above the sun, to carry His glory into a world trembling under chaos. Holy Spirit is whispering—urgent, unmistakable—a summons to rise as a beacon in this hour, fueling the billion-soul harvest, preparing the Bride for the King's return. The nations are waiting, and the throne room is beckoning you to shine.

The Journey We've Walked

We began at a worn table, feeling the weight of the world pressing heavy (Chapter 1). Elijah under the broom tree, Israel under Pharaoh's whip—we felt the futility of life under the sun. Yet Jesus promised: *"The one who endures to the end will be saved"* (Matthew 24:13).

Under the stars, we fought the battle of the mind (Chapter 2), tearing down strongholds with the Word. We learned to guard our eye gates, declaring, *"I am a new creation"* (2 Corinthians 5:17).

By the fireside, we discovered the law of beholding (Chapter 3)—that what you look at, you become. Fixing our eyes on Jesus, we were transformed from glory to glory (2 Corinthians 3:18).

At the table, Joseph walked with us (Chapter 4), showing that betrayal, injustice, and delay don't define us—God's presence does.

On the mountain trail, we embraced Spirit-led living (Chapter 5), aligning spirit, soul, and body, learning to shine in a world grown cold.

Back at the table, Esther called us higher (Chapter 6), rising for such a time as this, like Erika Kirk, who turned grief into revival's fire.

In the garden, we rested in the Father's love (Chapter 7), letting His embrace quiet our striving.

By the river, we walked in daily communion (Chapter 9), abiding in the Vine, keeping our lamps burning.

On the mountain peak, we surrendered our scrolls (Chapter 10), handing Him the pen to write His eternal purpose through our lives.

Now we stand in the throne room, where every chapter converges in one truth: the King is coming, and He is calling His Bride to live above the sun.

The Hour We're In

The world is shaking harder than ever. Headlines scream division. Truth is mocked. Love grows cold (Matthew 24:12). Social media amplifies chaos, pushing comparison, lust, and outrage. Young people chase identity in likes; adults numb themselves with distraction. Even the Church trembles, tempted to trade presence for performance.

But this is not the end. It is the beginning of the greatest awakening history has ever seen. I've witnessed the sparks: teenagers weeping for Jesus in school gyms, families praying through the night, churches overflowing with hunger no building can contain.

And persecution rises alongside it. Jesus warned: *"You will be hated by all for My name's sake"* (Matthew 24.9). The antichrist spirit seeks to silence truth-tellers—Charlie Kirk's assassination exposed this spirit—but the fire burning in Erika Kirk, and in you, cannot be quenched.

This is the hour of decision. Living above the sun is no longer optional—it is survival and destiny. Either drift with the noise, or burn with holy fire. The Bridegroom is at the door, and He is calling His Bride to be ready—without spot or wrinkle (Ephesians 5:27).

The Final Call: Shine His Glory

This is the call: live above the sun, carry the weight of His glory into the dark.

Every chapter has prepared you for this moment:

- **Reject the weight (Chapter 1):** Don't be crushed by chaos; lift your eyes to His throne.

- **Renew your mind (Chapter 2):** Break lies with truth, declaring His Word over strongholds.

- **Behold His glory (Chapter 3):** Fix your eyes on Jesus, becoming His image, glory to glory.

- **Endure like Joseph (Chapter 4):** Trust God's presence through betrayal, injustice, and delay.

- **Live Spirit-led (Chapter 5):** Align spirit, soul, and body to shine in a cold world.

- **Rise like Esther (Chapter 6):** Stand for such a time as this, carrying revival's fire.

- **Rest in His love (Chapter 7):** Let the Father's embrace quiet your striving.

- **Carry grief with wisdom (Chapter 8):** Remain seated with Christ while love and loss remain unresolved on the earth.

- **Abide in communion (Chapter 9):** Walk daily with Jesus, your lamp burning bright.

- **Rewrite your scroll (Chapter 10):** Surrender to God's purpose, living His eternal story.

This call isn't passive—it's warfare, a rebellion against the world's chaos. I've felt it, friend—moments when I faced the choice to drift in distraction or burn with holy fire. In a season of noise, I paused, prayed, and declared Revelation 22:17: *"Come, Lord Jesus!"* Peace came, not because the world quieted, but because my heart aligned with His purpose. I've seen it—a student, lost in social media's pull, surrendered to Christ and sparked a prayer movement; a family, fractured by stress, found healing in worship, their home a beacon. You're called to the same, friend—to shine, to stand, to carry His glory.

The Prophetic Fire: The Billion-Soul Harvest

I believe with everything in me that we stand at the edge of the billion-soul harvest. Prophets foresaw it. Holy Spirit is igniting it. It's already breaking out in hidden places—youth fasting in dorm rooms, parents interceding at kitchen tables, leaders preaching with fire that shakes cities.

This harvest is not for the lukewarm. It belongs to those whose lamps are full of the oil of intimacy. Those who have endured, abided, rested, risen, surrendered. Those who live above the sun.

"Behold, I am coming soon, bringing My recompense with Me" (Revelation 22:12). This is not a distant hope—it is the present

urgency of heaven. The trumpet is sounding. The fields are white. The Bridegroom is calling.

A Vision for the Rising Bride

I see it: a Bride rising, radiant with His glory, unbowed by the world's weight, unshaken by its lies. Her eyes are fixed on Jesus, her mind renewed, her spirit led, her heart resting in the Father's love. She walks in communion, her scroll rewritten, her life a testimony of His purpose.

She is young and old—students praying in gymnasiums, parents worshiping in their homes, churches blazing with revival. She carries Elijah's fire, Joseph's endurance, Esther's courage, and the Father's embrace.

This is not imagination—it is Revelation. *"The Bride has made herself ready."* (Revelation 19:7) And the Spirit and the Bride say, *"Come."* You are part of this Bride. You are called to join her song.

For Today: A Prophetic Invitation to Rise

The throne room is open, and the King is calling you to live above the sun. His glory outweighs the world's chaos. His purpose outshines its lies. This is your moment to say yes.

Here's the invitation I sense for you, straight from Holy Spirit's heart:

- Lift your eyes. Declare Psalm 121:1–2: *"I lift up my eyes to the hills… my help comes from the Lord."*

- Burn with fire. Reject lukewarmness; pray Revelation 3:16 for zeal.

- Shine His glory. Live as His light (Matthew 5:14).

- Join the harvest. Step out, speak truth, love boldly.

Let's pray together, simple and raw:

Lord Jesus, I say yes to You. Lift me above the sun. Renew my mind. Align my spirit. Rest my heart in Your love. Let my life shine Your glory, fuel Your harvest, and prepare Your Bride. Come, Lord Jesus—I am Yours. Amen.

The scroll has been opened, the trumpet is sounding, and the King is coming. **Live above the sun.**

Epilogue: The Benediction Above the Sun

And now may your spirit rise, carried by the wind of His presence. May your soul be anchored in His truth, and your body be a vessel of His glory. May the fire of endurance burn in you like Joseph, the courage of Esther steady you, the love of the Father hold you, and the oil of communion keep your lamp trimmed and full. May your scroll be rewritten by His hand, your steps ordered by His voice, and your life become a living testimony above the sun. The trumpet is sounding, the Bride is rising, and the King is coming. Stand ready, beloved—shine His glory until He breaks the skies.

Final Benediction — The Sound Above the Sun

The journey is complete, yet it has only begun.

Every word you've read, every revelation you've received, every whisper that stirred within you — all of it has been leading here. To this still point above the sun, where the veil thins and the King's glory burns brighter than the world's chaos.

You have walked through the valley of despair and stood on the mountain of destiny.

You have seen how endurance is forged in fire, how courage is birthed in surrender, and how intimacy is the truest form of victory.

You have beheld the heart of the Father, felt the breath of the Spirit, and glimpsed the ink of Heaven still writing upon your life.

Now the call resounds louder than ever:

Live above the sun.

Not as an escape from the world, but as a testimony to it.

To live above the sun is to think with Heaven's mind while walking through earth's dust.

It is to carry peace into panic, clarity into confusion, love into hatred, and truth into deception.

It is to become a walking tabernacle of presence — a dwelling place of the King.

This is your identity.

You are not defined by the fractures of your past or the noise of the present.

You are defined by the One who formed you, who breathed His Spirit into you, and who even now intercedes for you before the Father.

You are His beloved — spirit, soul, and body — restored, realigned, and reborn. Heaven is not silent. The scrolls are open. The Bride is awakening. The Spirit is moving across the waters of nations, hovering over chaos just as He did in the beginning — ready to speak again: *"Let there be light."*

And that light will shine through you. So rise, beloved. Carry the scroll of your story as a flame of witness. Guard your mind with truth. Fix your gaze on Jesus. Walk in step with the Spirit. Rest in the Father's embrace. Abide in communion daily. And let every breath become worship, every act become testimony, every word become light.

For you were not created to survive this world — you were sent to transform it. You were born to reveal the glory of the One who lives within you.

And when you walk above the sun, you carry Heaven's sound into the earth — the sound that heals minds, restores hearts, rewrites destinies, and prepares the Bride for the coming King.

And so I bless you: May your mind be renewed until it reflects the mind of Christ. May your heart burn with the unquenchable fire of His love. May your body become a vessel of light, healed and whole. May your life release the fragrance of Heaven wherever you go. May your scroll remain open in His hands until every word He dreamed over you is fulfilled. The trumpet is sounding. The harvest is ripening. The King is coming. Live ready. Live radiant. Live above the sun.

About the Author

Eric D. Cooper is a prophetic writer, teacher, and spiritual father whose life message is rooted in one conviction: *"I am a spirit being, that has a soul, that lives in a body. In Him I live and move and have my being."* His writings call a generation to live **above the sun**—beyond the chaos of the age—by walking in intimacy with Jesus, surrendering to the Holy Spirit, and embracing the Father's love.

Eric is the author of several books, including:

- *Set Your Mind on Things Above the Sun: How to Develop a Kingdom Mindset*

- *The Joseph Anointing: Living Above the Sun*

- *The Journey of Restoration: Rediscovering Hope in the Midst of Chaos*

- *Restoration Journey: A Daily Guide to Rebuilding Your Relationship with God through the Psalms and Proverbs*
- *I am Mad at Hell —I'm Not Taking It Anymore! Unveiling the Truths of Spiritual Warfare and Personal Empowerment*

- *Healing the Mind and Remembering Who You Are*

- *Above the Sun: A Prophetic Journey into God's Presence*

He is also the creator of *The Called Ones* series, a seven-part prophetic redemption novel written under the pen name **Aric Davian**. Blending narrative fire with prophetic revelation, the series speaks to spiritually orphaned youth, awakening their scrolls and calling them home.

Through his books, teachings, and legacy journaling project *Above the Sun: A Scroll of Restoration*, Eric's vision is to see generations reconciled, prodigals return, and a billion souls ignited by the fire of God's presence.

Reader's Blessing & Next Step

As you close these pages, may the Spirit breathe upon your heart with fresh wind and holy fire. May this not be the end of a book, but the beginning of your own restoration journey.

Take what the Lord has spoken to you here and begin to walk it out—one prayer, one whisper, one act of obedience at a time.

Write your own scroll. Listen for His voice. Live above the sun.

To continue your journey, explore Above the Sun: A Scroll of Restoration—a living journal of prophetic reflection, legacy letters, and communion with the Father.

You can follow future writings, teachings, and resources at EricCooper.com or AboveTheSun.ca, where the story continues and the scrolls keep unfolding.

Invitation To Connect

If this book has stirred something deep in your spirit—if you've wept, wrestled, or awakened to fresh purpose—then I want you to know: this journey doesn't end with the last page.

I'd be honored to hear your story.

Whether you're walking through a pit, rising from a prison, or standing at the threshold of purpose, your voice matters. This message of reformation is not just a book—it's a movement of sons and daughters stepping into their God-given destiny. And I believe you're one of them.

Let's stay connected. Let's grow together. Let's keep dreaming— *above the sun.*

You can find new teachings, prophetic insights, and ministry updates at:

- www.TheJosephAnointing.com
- www.ericcooper.com
- Email: contact@ericcooper.com
- Instagram: @abovethesunbooks
- Faccbook: @EricCooperAuthor

You were born for reformation. Let's walk it out—together.

With honor,

Eric D. Cooper

Books by Eric D. Cooper

Set Your Mind on Things Above the Sun

How to Develop a Kingdom Mindset

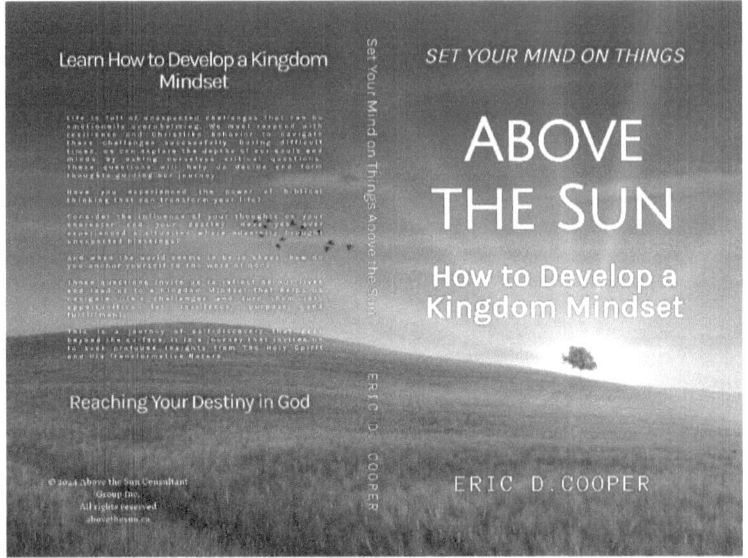

Available in English, Spanish, and Portuguese

A transformative journey into intentional focus and spiritual empowerment, equipping readers with Biblical principles to live a purpose-driven life rooted in a Kingdom mindset.

I Am Mad at Hell—I'm Not Taking It Anymore!

Unveiling the Truths of Spiritual Warfare and Personal Empowerment

Available in English and Spanish

A bold guide to overcoming spiritual attacks and adversity through faith, offering practical strategies and inspiring testimonies to live a victorious life.

The Journey of Restoration

Rediscovering Hope in the Midst of Chaos – A

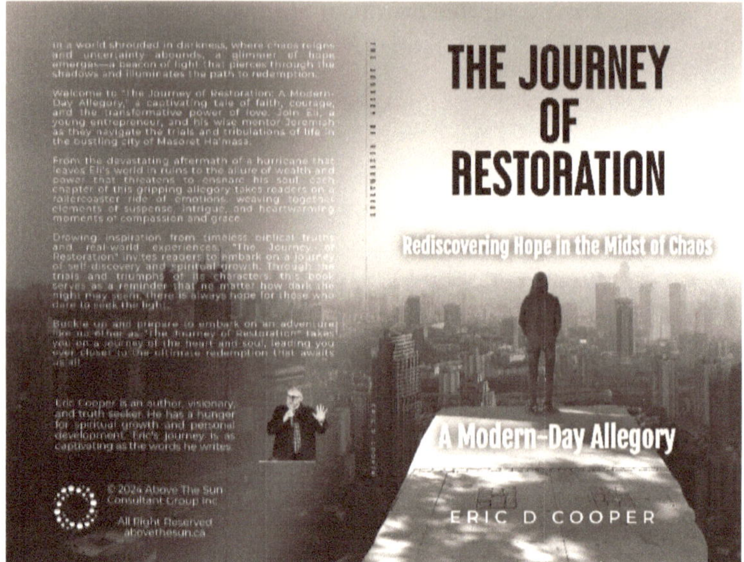

Modern-Day Allegory

Available in English

*A compelling Biblical allegory following Eli's journey through trials
in Masoret Ha'masa, reflecting themes of resilience, redemption, and
hope.*

Restoration Journey

A Daily Guide to Rebuilding Your Relationship with God through the Psalms and Proverbs

Available in English, Spanish, and Portuguese

A 30-day devotional guiding readers through Psalms and Proverbs to renew their relationship with God, with reflections, prayers, and practical applications.

ABOVE
THE SUN
How to Develop a
Kingdom Mindset
ERIC D. COOPER

RESTORATION
THE JOURNEY
OF
RESTORATION
A Modern-Day Allegory
ERIC D COOPER

ERIC D COOPER
I AM
MAD AT
HELL
I'M NOT TAKING
IT ANYMORE!

Aprenda Como Desenvolver uma
Mentalidade do Reino

SUA MENTE NAS COISAS

ACIMA
DO SOL

Como Desenvolver uma
Mentalidade do Reino

ERIC D. COOPER

Tradução por Luanna Monteiro

Alcançando Seu Destino em Deus

© 2024 Above the Sun Consultant Group Inc.
Todos os direitos reservados
abovethesun.ca

Aprende a Desarrollar una Mentalidad del Reino

La vida está llena de desafíos inesperados que pueden ser emocionalmente abrumadores. Debemos responder con resiliencia y un comportamiento semejante a Cristo para navegar exitosamente estos desafíos. Durante los tiempos difíciles, podemos explorar las profundidades de nuestras almas y mentes haciéndonos preguntas difíciles. Estas preguntas nos ayudarán a decidir y formar pensamientos que guían nuestro camino.

¿Has experimentado el poder del pensamiento bíblico que puede transformar tu vida?

Considera la influencia de tus pensamientos en tu carácter y tu destino. ¿Alguna vez has experimentado una situación en la que la adversidad trajo condiciones inesperadas?

Y cuando el mundo parece estar en caos, ¿cómo te anclas en la Palabra de Dios?

Estas preguntas nos invitan a reflexionar sobre nuestras vidas y nos conducen a una Mentalidad del Reino que nos ayuda a enfrentar los desafíos de la vida y convertirlos en oportunidades de resiliencia, propósito y plenitud.

Esta es un viaje de autodescubrimiento que va más allá de lo superficial. Es un viaje que nos invita a buscar profundos conocimientos del Espíritu Santo y su Naturaleza Transformadora.

Alcanzando Tu Destino en Dios

© 2024 Above the Sun Consultant Group Inc.
Todos los derechos reservados
abovethesun.ca

Enfoca tu Mente en las Cosas Más Allá del Sol

ERIC D. COOPER

ENFOCA TU MENTE EN LAS COSAS

MÁS ALLÁ DEL SOL

Cómo desarrollar una Mentalidad del Reino

ERIC D. COOPER

Traducido por Briant Guzmán

Revelando las verdades de la guerra espiritual y el empoderamiento personal

¿Se siente abrumado por los ataques espirituales o aturdido por las grandes pérdidas infligidas por el maligno? "Estoy enojado con el infierno, ya no lo soportaré más" ofrece un rayo de esperanza y empoderamiento específicamente para usted.

El autor Eric Cooper expone sin miedo los planes insidiosos del enemigo, revelando cómo el diablo busca robar, matar y destruir los destinos de los creyentes en Cristo. Pero este libro es más que una simple exposición, es un manifiesto de guerra espiritual y empoderamiento personal, diseñado para ayudarte a recuperar tu victoria.

En su interior descubrirás:

• Perspectivas sobre la guerra espiritual: obtenga una comprensión más profunda de las tácticas del enemigo y cómo combatirlas con sabiduría bíblica.
• Estrategias prácticas para la victoria: aprenda siete consejos esenciales arraigados en las Escrituras para ayudarte a desarrollar un carácter piadoso y superar los desafíos de la vida.
• Testimonios de Triunfo: historias inspiradoras de personas que enfrentaron la adversidad de frente y salieron victoriosos a través del poder de la fe.

Eric Cooper es un líder, mentor y maestro profético apasionado por ayudar a las personas a descubrir su propósito en Cristo. Con más de cuatro décadas de experiencia, el estilo de liderazgo de Eric combina de manera única sabiduría, visión profética, calidez y compasión.

© Copyright 2024 ABOVE THE SUN CONSULTANT GROUP INC. Todos los derechos reservados
abovethesun.ca

ERIC D COOPER

ESTOY ENOJADO CON EL INFIERNO ¡NO LO ESTOY TOMANDO MÁS!

ERIC D COOPER

ESTOY ENOJADO CON EL INFIERNO

NO VOY A SOPORTARLO MÁS

Revelando las verdades de la guerra espiritual y el empoderamiento personal

VIAJE DE RESTAURACIÓN
Una guía para reconstruir tu relación con Dios a través de los Salmos y Proverbios
VIAJE DE RESTAURACIÓN
Una guía para reconstruir tu relación con Dios a través de los Salmos y Proverbios
ERIC D COOPER
Traducido por Briant Guzmán
ERIC D COOPER

ERIC COOPER

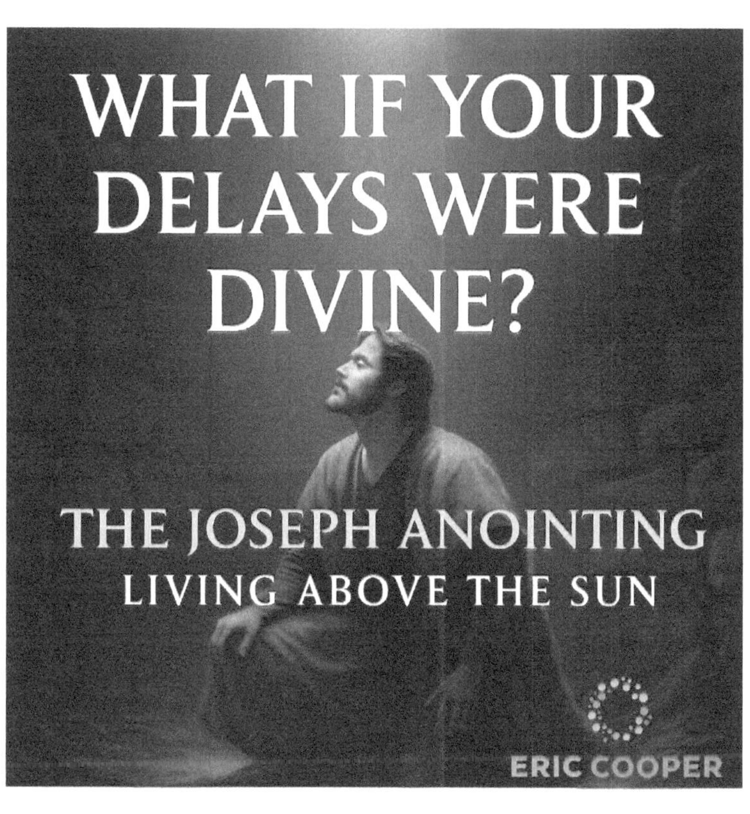
WHAT IF YOUR
DELAYS WERE
DIVINE?

THE JOSEPH ANOINTING
LIVING ABOVE THE SUN

ERIC COOPER

ABOVE THE SUN
CONSULTANT GROUP